IN CONCERT

ELVIS

BUILDING
PERSONNEL

IN CONCERT

ELVIS

BUILDING
PERSONNEL

ELVIS
BY THE PRESLEYS

ELVIS
BY THE PRESLEYS

Edited by David Ritz
Design by Ruba Abu-Nimah
Still-Life Photography by Henry Leutwyler

Crown Publishers
New York

David Ritz has collaborated on the memoirs of, among others, Ray Charles, Marvin Gaye, BB King, Aretha Franklin, Etta James, Smokey Robinson and the Neville Brothers. His lyrics include "Sexual Healing." Ritz is a four-time winner of the Ralph J. Gleason/Rolling Stone Music Book Award.

Ruba Abu-Nimah's vision as an art director or a conceptor has shaped the brands and communications of Calvin Klein, Jennifer Lopez, Nate Berkus, Rocco DiSpirito, Courtney Love, Estée Lauder, Max Factor, Henri Bendel and Marc Jacobs among others. Abu-Nimah's past work has received innumerable awards, including the Art Directors Club, *How* magazine and PDN.

Henry Leutwyler is an internationally acclaimed photographer whose work has appeared in *The New York Times Magazine*, *Vogue*, *Vanity Fair* and *Esquire*. Among his subjects are His Majesty King Abdullah of Jordan, Elvis Costello, Nathan Lane, Wim Wenders, Mikhail Gorbachev, Oprah Winfrey, Tom Wolfe and Dizzy Gillespie.

Published in the United States by Crown Publishers, an imprint of the Crown Publishing Group, a division of Random House, Inc., New York.
www.crownpublishing.com

Library of Congress Cataloging-in-Publication Data
is available upon request

ISBN 0-307-23741-9

Printed in the United States of America

10 9 8 7 6 5 4 3 2 1

First Edition

DEEP GRATITUDE TO THE WITNESSES:

Ann

Lisa Marie

Michelle

Patsy

Paul

Priscilla

SPECIAL THANKS TO EPE:

LaVonne Gaw

Kelly Hill

Gary Hovey

Michelle Beaulieu Hovey

Sheila James

Angie Marchese

Todd Morgan

Susan Sherwood

Jack Soden

And all the staff of Elvis Presley Enterprises, Inc.

THANKS, TOO, GO TO:

Luke Dempsey

Paige Dorian

Matthias Gaggl

Elisabeth Harris

Teresa Horgan

Anisha Kansal

Ross Kasovitz

Kenneth Kraus

Sebastian Kriete

Jason Jamal Nakleh

Rebecca Omweg

Elisa Petrini

David Saltz

Jerry Schilling

David Vigliano

Lisa Marie Presley interviews are taken from the
television special and DVD *Elvis by the Presleys*

JŌVAN
musk oil
aftershave/cologne
for MEN.
4 FL. OZ.
JOVAN, INC. CHICAGO, ILL. 60611

Record player from Elvis's bedroom and the album that was on it the day he passed away

Elvis's walking stick with knife handle

ELVIS

Taking Care of Business

THE FAMILY

Priscilla Beaulieu Presley (Elvis's former wife)

Lisa Marie Presley (Elvis and Priscilla's daughter)

Patsy Presley Geranen (Elvis's double first cousin*)

Ann Beaulieu (Priscilla's mother)

Paul Beaulieu (Priscilla's father)

Michelle Beaulieu Hovey (Priscilla's sister)

*Brothers — Elvis's dad Vernon and Patsy's dad Vester — married sisters —
Elvis's mom Gladys and Patsy's mom Clettes.

Chapter One

ELVIS IS IN THE HOUSE

PRISCILLA: Who can think of Elvis without thinking of Graceland? Walk through the front door and you feel him. He's here. Here in spirit and here in memory. With all his music and movies, with all the stories surrounding his life, there may never have been a more public man than Elvis Presley. But behind the gates of Graceland, Elvis was an extremely private man who lived an extremely private life.

To understand Elvis — the real Elvis — is to see him in his truest element. That's Graceland.

PATSY: Graceland is Elvis's heart. It's where he was most himself and where he felt most loved. It's where he returned, time and time again, from all his great adventures — movies in Hollywood, shows in Las Vegas, concerts in Hawaii.

I worked in the office at Graceland with Elvis's dad, Uncle Vernon. Elvis was not only my cousin, he was my boss, but mainly he was my brother. From the time we were little kids in Mississippi to the day he died, we had a close and loving relationship.

In Elvis's mind, he always associated Graceland with his mother, my aunt Gladys. In 1957, he bought the big estate for her. Remember, we were Depression poor people from Tupelo. When Elvis's records got popular, among the first things he did was buy Aunt Gladys a pink Cadillac, pretty dresses and nice jewelry. He wanted to buy her the world. All his life he dreamed of making her comfortable. Graceland was that dream come true. The tragedy was that she lived there barely a year before she died in 1958. Her death shocked us all. Elvis was devastated. No one could console him. She was his life.

ELVIS: Everyone loves their mother, but I was an only child and Mother was always right there with me. All my life. It wasn't like losing a mother, it was like losing a friend, a companion, someone to talk to. I could wake her up any hour of the night if I was worried or troubled by something. She'd get up and try to help me.

PATSY: I never saw a more loving relationship between a mother and son. Aunt Gladys was full of fun and energy. She brought out the best in Elvis. He

Gladys's jewelry box

Elvis's personally engraved money clip

Elvis's gold-plated Barretta

inherited her vitality and humor. When Gladys was around, Elvis was never down or depressed. When Elvis was away, Gladys was never relaxed. She worried something would happen to her boy. The bond between them was so close no one could get in between. Gladys gave Elvis the confidence he needed to go out into the world. When she left the world, he didn't know what to do.

Maybe it was a good thing that he had to go back to the army where he was sent over to Germany. Being at Graceland right after his mother passed might have been too much to bear.

His homecoming in 1960 was wonderful. Graceland was exciting again. Graceland was alive again. I could see he was thrilled to be home. But I also felt his sadness. I felt how much he missed his mother. For all the wonderful times at Graceland — all the meals and parties and games and birthdays and holidays — Graceland was never the same after Aunt Gladys passed. Elvis was never the same.

PRISCILLA: When Elvis and I met in Germany a few months before the end of his army stint, he kept describing Graceland to me — how much I would love it, and how much his mother would have loved me were she still alive. He pined for his home and he pined for his mother. I was a young girl then — only fourteen — and couldn't begin to understand the importance that Graceland held in Elvis's heart. As years went by, though, as I myself lived in Graceland and Graceland became part of my own heart, I understood that it was much more than a place. It was Elvis's refuge from the storms of life. It was where he dreamt of raising a family and finding simple peace.

Gold-plated phone from Elvis's bedroom

Remote control from Elvis's bedroom, 1957

Sometimes he found that peace, sometimes he didn't, but he never stopped trying. Graceland symbolized his hopes for a happy life. That's why he always came home.

PATSY: When Elvis was in Germany he wrote a beautiful letter to me and my parents. He described being in the mountains on maneuvers. It was freezing cold. His detail was demanding. He felt himself getting sick with a sore throat and chills. He said he had never been so homesick in his life. He wrote about the one Christmas when we were all together at Graceland, when Aunt Gladys was still alive, and how he cherished that memory. He went on about the importance of family in his life. For Elvis, family was everything. You couldn't read the letter without crying. You couldn't read it without feeling Elvis's sensitivity. Of all the many things Elvis left us with, I value that letter above everything. It showed how deeply he loved his home.

LISA MARIE: I was born in 1968 and have enough memories of Graceland to keep my head spinning for the rest of my life. It was amazing. Filled with energy and excitement. Always something going on. Non-stop action. And surprises. Of course it was all about my father. It was his energy and excitement that kept us all on our toes. If he was in a good mood, it was going to be a great day. We'd ride horses or ride around in golf carts. The kitchen was Grand Central. Something was always cooking. Because my father was nocturnal, Pauline and Lottie, the night cooks, were always on call. The day cooks, Nancy and Mary, had to keep an eye on me. Everyone had to keep an eye on me. If I was scared at night, Pauline would sit by my bed. Food was a big part of Graceland.

My father's family was southern and so was the food. Comfort food. Ham and eggs. Pounds of bacon.

PRISCILLA: The attic in Graceland seemed to call to me. Elvis's paternal grandmother, Minnie Mae, who lived with us in Graceland, claimed she heard noises coming from Gladys's ghost. Well, I didn't believe in ghosts and was determined to see exactly what was up there. One day while Elvis was off making a movie in Hollywood, I ventured upstairs. I can't say I wasn't apprehensive. It was a stormy afternoon. Heavy rain. Thunder and lightning. I slowly opened the attic door. It creaked like it hadn't been opened in years. Inside, it was pitch dark. I took a couple of steps forward and found the light switch. The yellow bulb lit a long line of clothing racks. These were Gladys's clothes. Elvis had saved everything. All her precious belongings were here. I could feel her spirit. I was excited and moved. One by one, I examined her blouses, skirts and dresses. They were simple, not extravagant, and gave me a sense of her character. It might sound strange, but I would bring these articles of clothing to my face and breathe in their essence. I knew this was as close as I would get to Elvis's beloved mother. I tried on a couple of coats. It was as though she were embracing me. And just as I was lost in a reverie, thinking of how this charismatic woman shaped my husband's charismatic personality, the door flew open. I screamed! Seeing me, the woman who had opened the door screamed even louder! It was Hattie, one of our housekeepers. She was certain she'd seen a ghost. It took us several minutes to get our bearings. When we finally did, we were able to laugh, but the experience of discovering Gladys's wardrobe and feeling her presence was something that lives within me to this day.

**TV from Elvis's house
in Palm Springs**

One of Elvis's
favorite colognes

PRISCILLA: Elvis was always stunning. Appearance was important to him. He loved clothes. He loved fine fabrics. Outside of his movie roles, he never wore jeans because as a poor kid all he had were jeans. Even at home, even on casual days, he'd wear a beautiful silk shirt and tailored trousers. He always made a strong and compelling visual impression.

LISA MARIE: You'd hear him before you'd see him. You'd hear these noises at the top of the staircase. He'd slowly make his way down, and there he was. The thing about my father is that he never hid anything. He didn't have a façade. Never put on airs. If he was crabby, you knew it. If he was angry, he'd let you know. His temper could give Darth Vader a run for his money. But if he was happy, everyone was happy. He had that kind of charisma. He'd never bore you.

One morning after breakfast he gets up and says, "Lisa, come outside. There's something I want to show you." I run after him and right there in the backyard is a pony. "It's yours," he says, "all yours." He lifts me up and puts me on the pony. He starts leading me around the yard and back into the house. As we pass by my great-grandmother's room, the pony decides to relieve himself. Now my great-grandmother starts yelling, "What's all the commotion

about?" "Oh, it's nothing, Dodger" — that's his nickname for her — "nothing at all." My father is extremely respectful of her, and maybe a little afraid of her, so he's running me and the pony down the hallway, through the dining room and back out the door. Fortunately, she doesn't move too quickly and the mess gets mopped up before she opens her door. The whole house — his friends, the maids, the cooks, his dad, everyone — was always waiting for my father's next move. You never knew when that would be. His insomnia turned time upside down. I remember mentioning how much I wanted a puppy. Next thing I know it's 3 a.m. and my father has organized a caravan of cars and we're rolling past the gates of Graceland to some pet store where the owner opens up in the middle of the night for this crew of twenty people. That night all twenty people get puppies.

PRISCILLA: There were two universes — the normal universe and the universe of Elvis. Once you got a taste of Elvis's universe, you didn't want to leave it. You realized it was a privilege to be invited in and you did all you could to stay there. That meant staying in his good graces. And showing him loyalty. Nothing was more important to Elvis than loyalty.

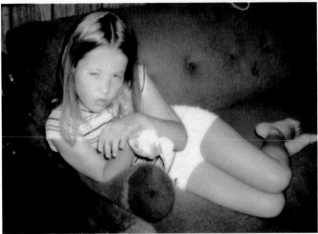

Graceland was the perfect expression of Elvis's universe because it existed closest to his roots. Graceland is where he first figured out how to be most comfortable. He loved having his boys around him, loved having his dad and cousin Patsy running the office, loved the familiarity of a world he controlled. Even the fans at the gate — who were always there — reminded him of his tremendous popularity while reminding us how lucky we were. We were inside. And inside Graceland is where everyone wanted to be.

Priscilla, her mom and brother in the kitchen at Graceland (top)
Lisa Marie in The Jungle Room at Graceland (middle)
Elvis in the music room (bottom)

25

Bracelet from Elvis's collection, circa 1972

Original mailbox at Graceland

3764

HWY. 51

Delta (standing),
Dodger and Lisa Marie

DELTA AND DODGER IN THE HOUSE THAT NEVER SLEPT

PATSY: Elvis was king of the castle — no doubt — but his rule did not extend to my grandmother and my aunt.

Grandma was Minnie Mae, Vernon and my dad's mom. Because she and her husband split up early on, she came to live with Vernon, Gladys and Elvis even before they came to Memphis. Minnie Mae was the matriarch. Minnie Mae liked attention. I called her Mamaw, but Elvis called her Dodger because she had successfully dodged a ball he'd thrown at her as a kid.

LISA MARIE: I have this mental picture of Dodger: her hair up in a bun, wearing funky glasses, watching "Hee Haw" and dipping into her snuff. She was always dipping into her snuff.

PATSY: She had a snuff box and a little hickory brush. She'd dip the brush in the snuff and put it in her mouth. She wouldn't wear teeth. I'd find her teeth in her purse. I'd find her teeth all over the house. She liked dresses with ruffles and every day of her life wore an ornate apron tied around her waist. She said she couldn't hear well, but if you'd whisper something about her on the other side of the house she'd hear you. Elvis adored her and she adored him. For all her quirks, she was a good listener. You could go to her with your troubles. She wasn't judgmental or harsh. Mamaw was very wise.

PRISCILLA: I first met her when she was living with Elvis and his dad in Germany. I didn't really know her then, but later on we became so close that when Elvis was away from Graceland I'd sleep in her room. Her sense of survival was a comfort. Her strength made us all stronger.

PATSY: Our aunt Delta, Minnie Mae's daughter, came to Graceland in the mid-Sixties to care for her mother. Her husband Pat, who had been a riverboat gambler, had died. Family talk was that Pat and Delta had lived the wild life all across the country in casinos and bars. There was a mystique about them, a mysterious past that no one could detail. All I know is this: when aunt Delta arrived at Graceland, the place was never the same.

PRISCILLA: I still see Delta: walking around the grounds in her nightgown, rollers in her hair; shooting the finger to the tourists at the gate; cursing like a sailor; feeding her nasty dog four kinds of gourmet food.

LISA MARIE: Delta's dog, Edmund, is the dog out of *Omen*. The dog from hell.

PRISCILLA: No dog has ever been treated better than Edmund. She pampered him like a baby. I remember thinking, *If I ever come back, I'd like to come back as one of Delta's dogs.*

PATSY: One day I looked out the window of the office and saw Aunt Delta throwing lit matches on something that looked like a bird's nest. What in the world was she burning in the middle of the day?

When I went into the house as usual after work, I asked her what she had burned. She told me it was her wig.

"Why in God's name did you burn your wig?"

"Someone liked it and asked me for it. I'm just making sure she doesn't get it."

"Why would she do that?"

"She can't," said Delta, looking at the wig that was now burned to a crisp.

She looked at me and we just laughed. She was a real prize.

LISA MARIE: Delta was a diabetic alcoholic. The woman was hysterically funny. She'd insult anyone who'd come within a five-mile radius of her. People feared her.

The gun Delta carried with her

A small sampling of Delta's Harlequin romance collection

11/89	49	HAZARDOUS ASSIGNMENT Stafford	373-17049-1-250
11/89	3017	TROUBLEMAKER Ker	373-03017-7-250
11/89	3018	UNWILLING WOMAN Peters	373-03018-5-250
12/89	1228	don't ask why **ANNABEL MURRAY**	373-11228-9-250
12/89	1230	unwilling heart **EMMA RICHMOND**	373-11230-0-250
11/89	1218	wild justice **JOANNA MANSELL**	373-11218-1-250
11/89	1217	not without love **ROBERTA LEIGH**	373-11217-3-250
11/89	1216	lovers touch **PENNY JORDAN**	373-11216-5-250
12/89	1229	man without a past **VALERIE PARV**	373-11229-7-250
12/89	3021	LETTERS OF LOVE Kaye	373-03021-5-250
11/89	3014	LOVING DECEIVER Arthur	373-03014-2-250
7/89		*Through Eyes of Love*	
12/89	3020	FOLLY TO LOVE Jacobs	373-03020-7-250
12/89	52	A SECRET TRUTH York	373-17052-1-250
7/89	1187	prisoner of the mind **MARGARET MAYO**	373-11187-8-250
7/89	1186	the third kiss **JOANNA MANSELL**	373-11186-X-250
12/89	3019	THE SNOW GARDEN Campbell	373-03019-3-250

Among the fans, she even got a little famous. One fan asked her, "Aren't you Aunt Delta?" "Hell, no," she snapped back. "Aunt Delta's dead. The old hag died last night."

You had to love Delta. I know she loved me. She was the only one at Graceland who'd drive me to the 7/11 for candy. She'd run over curbs and run down people on the streets. She'd try to make me take a bath — I hated baths, I wouldn't bathe for days—and come after me, screaming, "You little bastard, you little s.o.b.!" She never did catch me. Only one person could get me in the tub, and that was my father. He was generous. He loved watching people's faces light up and freak out when he gave them stuff—cars and jewelry and horses and anything else you can imagine. He loved giving. So it makes sense that the happiest time of year for him was Christmas.

PATSY: Uncle Vernon was Santa. With his bright blue eyes and cotton-wool beard, he was perfect. Lisa Marie was convinced that he was actually jolly ole St. Nick just in from the North Pole. Elvis loved Christmas at Graceland. Christmas let him forget all the pressures of his career.

PRISCILLA: Elvis was sentimental, and Christmas brought out his sentiments in force. He loved decorative lights, for example, and kept getting more and more. Oddly enough, he got the idea from the way the mansions in Beverly Hills and Bel Air were lit for Christmas. On the lawn in front of Graceland we had a Santa and sleigh and later an elaborate nativity scene. When it snowed one Christmas, Elvis was in heaven. We ran out and built a giant snowman. He made snow ice cream, a favorite treat. He became a

little boy all over again, which, of course, was one of his most endearing qualities. The little boy in Elvis was always ready to go out and play.

LISA MARIE: One time in the middle of the night I'm awoken by this incredibly loud noise coming from my father's bedroom, which was right next to mine. I get out of bed and see the guys buzz-sawing down his door so they can move in a grand piano. He felt like playing piano and singing gospel songs. Gospel was his favorite and around Christmas he sang it all the time. Those were the songs he learned as a kid.

PATSY: Elvis was brought up in the Assembly of God church. His mom and dad were believers and regular church goers in Tupelo. It was a musical church and God's music got in Elvis's soul early on.

ELVIS: My mother and dad both love to sing. They tell me when I was three or four I got away from them in church and I walked up in front of the choir and started beating time.

PRISCILLA: In the piano room, just back off the living room, Elvis and his dad would sing "Precious Lord" or "Amazing Grace." Vernon had a good voice, and nothing calmed Elvis like harmonizing to the songs he was raised up on. Gospel music was his deepest roots and, I believe, his deepest love.

LISA MARIE: My father was always singing songs, playing the piano or guitar or listening to music. One Christmas I remember wanting music of my own. I asked for Elton John albums. Well, my father wouldn't get them. But Aunt Delta, who couldn't care less what her nephew thought, went out and got them.

45

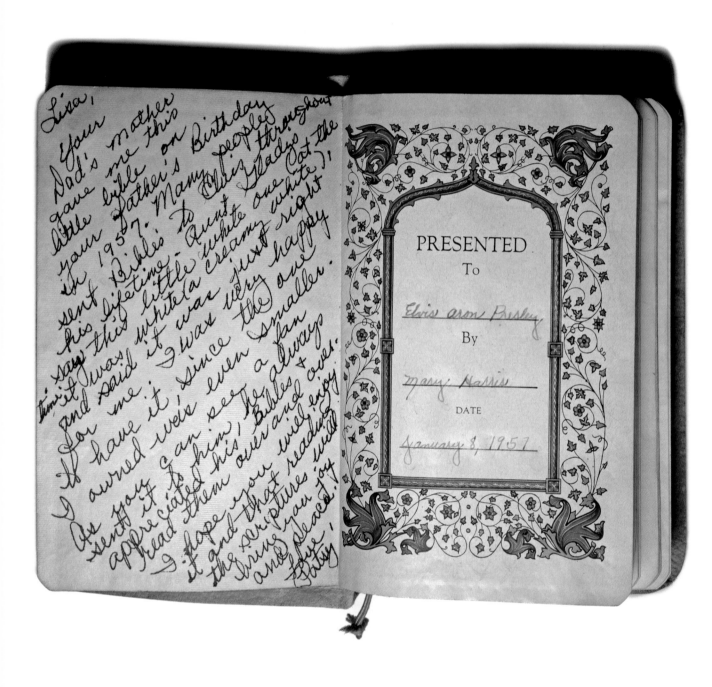

Lisa,

Your Dad's mother gave me this little bible on your Father's Birthday in 1957. Many peoples sent Bibles to Elvis throughout his lifetime. Aunt Gladys say this little white one for me. It was white (a creamy white) and said it was very happy to have it. I was just happy I owned it. Since the one as you can see it is even smaller sent it to him, the always appreciated his Bibles + read them over and over. I hope you will enjoy it and that reading the scripture will bring you much joy and peace!

Patsy!

PRESENTED

To

Elvis aron Presley

By

Mary Harris

DATE

January 8, 1957

A bible given to Elvis from a fan. Gladys then gave it to Patsy who, in turn, gave it to Lisa Marie many years later.

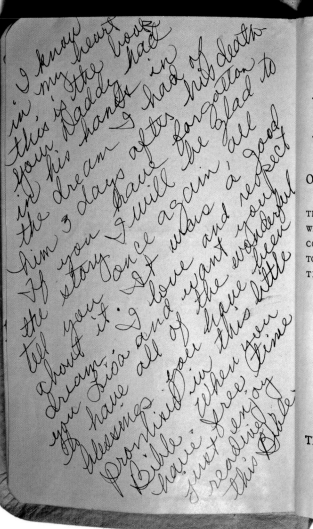

in... I know in my heart
this is the book
your Daddy had
in his hands in
the dream I had of
him 3 days after his death.
If you have forgotten
tell your once again, all
about it. It was a good
dream. I love and respect
you Lisa and want you to
have all of the wonderful
blessings God have in this little
promised in this Bible when your
have time free. Just enjoy
reading this Bible.

THE
Holy Bible

CONTAINING THE

OLD AND NEW TESTAMENTS

TRANSLATED OUT OF THE ORIGINAL TONGUES;
WITH THE FORMER TRANSLATIONS DILIGENTLY
COMPARED AND REVISED &⁊ CONFORMABLE
TO THE EDITION OF 1611, COMMONLY KNOWN AS
THE AUTHORIZED OR KING JAMES VERSION

SELF-PRONOUNCING EDITION

THE WORLD PUBLISHING COMPANY

CLEVELAND AND NEW YORK

Christmas card, 1957

ELVIS: My favorite style of music is spiritual music. Why I know practically every religious song that's ever been written.

LISA MARIE: So there we all are, Christmas morning, sitting under the tree and opening presents. But as soon as I unwrap my Elton John records, my father grabs them and starts saying, "Who is this guy?" and "Why should my daughter be listening to him and not me?" The truth is that I did listen to his records all the time, and I loved them. It's just that this new guy's music caught my ear. Wasn't long after that, though, that my father came around and started listening to Elton himself. He even went to an Elton concert. That same Christmas we went sledding. It was icy and I was a little nervous. So my father pulled my sled along rather than let me take off on my own. Then he gets on a sled, lays flat on his stomach, and aims for the steepest part of the driveway. He's racing down the driveway when he hits the curb, flies off the sled and lands on his stomach. We wait for him to get up, but he's not moving. He's laid out there like he's dead. I start to scream. The boys come running. When we get to him someone says, "Don't touch him before we call a doctor." He's still not moving. Doesn't even look like he's breathing when suddenly he jumps up and starts laughing.

PRISCILLA: It was another Christmas at Graceland when Elvis called me outside and presented me with a beautiful black quarter horse named Domino. I loved Domino and began riding every day. At first Elvis was a little fearful of horses, but he saw I was having such a great time he wanted to join. That was the start of his Great Horse Phase. Elvis never did anything halfway. He became totally obsessed with whatever he was doing, and, believe me, this Great Horse Phase was intense. He decided he had to have a Golden Palomino and thus began the search. We'd run around the countryside, from horse farm to horse farm, knocking on doors in the middle of night to see if there were any Golden Palominos for sale. You'd think people would be annoyed, but when they saw it was Elvis they were thrilled. Didn't matter that

Christmas card, 1966

it was four in the morning. Finally we found the horse, a breathtakingly gorgeous animal — Rising Sun — and naturally Elvis became a superb rider.

But it wasn't enough that Elvis and I had horses. All the gang had to have horses. Elvis bought horses for everyone — the guys, the guys' wives, every family member and friend. And not only did he buy everyone horses, he bought custom saddles and blankets and stirrups. He transformed Graceland's barn into a fully functioning horse barn. He had us painting the stalls, painting the names of the horses on the stalls and color-coordinating every imaginable piece of gear. It was a little crazy but, like most everything with Elvis, it was a lot of fun.

PATSY: There's a famous story about Elvis and Rising Sun. You see, Rising Sun was a lot like Elvis. Stubborn. Rebellious. Did what he wanted to do when he wanted to do it. One afternoon they were out riding when Rising

Sun threw Elvis. Elvis landed flat on his backside. He didn't like that. Elvis looked at him and hit him right between the eyes, dazing Rising Sun. Rising Sun never threw him again.

PRISCILLA: In my mind I often go back to Graceland. It was a lifestyle unlike any other. The power of Elvis's personality dominated our every day. Every day was different. And so were the nights. He might rent out the Memphian movie theater and have us watch four features in a row. Or rent out the skating rink and have us compete like crazy. Or close down the fairground so we could ride the rollercoaster till daybreak. Elvis might do anything.

In between the excitement, though, on a rainy day in winter or a fragrant night in spring, I'd find myself asking questions: *What wildly improbable forces conspired to link my life with his? How in the world did I ever find my way to Graceland?*

Elvis's saddle

Elvis's boot, with the original mud

ELVIS
IN
CONCERT
SPECIAL
Guest Artist

ELVIS
IN
PERSON
396

ELVIS

ELVIS
SHOW MEMBER

Concert buttons from the Seventies

Chapter Three

FATE

PAUL BEAULIEU: I suppose it all started at the PX in Austin, Texas. As a career Air Force officer, I was doing a little shopping when I noticed a long line of people buying a record album. I went over and saw the name — Elvis Presley — and wasn't even sure how to pronounce it. Anyway, I thought it might be something my daughter Priscilla would like, so I bought it for her. It seemed like music for her generation.

PRISCILLA: I liked the music, I *loved* "Blue Suede Shoes," but I was hardly fanatic. I was a twelve-year-old kid, skinny and shy, who didn't want to be part of the Elvis mania. In fact, I refused to join the Elvis fan club — admission 25 cents — when I learned that one member had asked Elvis to autograph her breast. In my pre-teen mind, that was too risqué. On the other hand, I liked Elvis enough to want to watch him on the Ed Sullivan show.

ANN BEAULIEU: We had reservations about Priscilla watching that show. This was 1956, when our world was quite conservative. I can't say I had a high opinion of this rock and roll.

PAUL: Frankly, we forbade her to watch the show. We sent her to her room.

PRISCILLA: Forbidden fruit is that much sweeter. I cracked open my door just enough to see the television set. Say whatever you like about Elvis, but he was a thrilling performer.

PAUL: A couple of years later I was transferred to West Germany. Priscilla was a popular girl in her junior high, and I knew this would be difficult for her, but we had no choice.

PRISCILLA: I was crushed. The last thing I wanted was to leave my friends and go off to some frozen foreign country. One of my schoolmates mentioned Elvis. Since his first album, his fame had grown. He was starring in movies — *Love Me Tender, Jailhouse Rock, King Creole.* "Elvis is in the army over there," the friend said. "Maybe you'll run into him." "Oh sure," I replied.

I was miserable in Wiesbaden. I'd been there only three weeks but missed Austin terribly. I spent all my spare time at the Eagles Club, a place where American service families hung out. I'd go there to write long letters to my friends back home. One afternoon I was there with my little sister and brother when a serviceman happened to strike up a conversation with me. He was an especially nice guy who sensed that I was homesick. "Would you like to meet Elvis Presley?" he asked. "Who wouldn't like to meet Elvis," I answered. I thought he was kidding but he wasn't. His name was Currie Grant and he said that he and his wife often visited Elvis, who lived forty-five minutes away in the town of Bad Nauheim.

PAUL: We were skeptical at first, but after meeting Currie Grant and his wife we saw they were sincere and responsible people. When Ann and I talked it over, we also remembered something Priscilla said when we went shopping in Frankfurt. "Wouldn't it be fun if we saw Elvis on the street?" Cilla was a young girl in tune with the young world. How could we deny her something which she'd remember her whole life? Besides, we were assured that there'd be plenty of chaperones.

PRISCILLA: I wore a blue-and-white sailor dress, and I was petrified. The drive seemed to take forever. I didn't open my mouth. When we finally arrived, the first person I met was Vernon, Elvis's dad. He couldn't have been nicer. He led us to the crowded living room where Brenda Lee was singing "Sweet Nothin's" on the record player. And there he was.

He was wearing a red sweater and tan slacks. He was breathtakingly handsome, far more handsome than

On "The Ed Sullivan Show," 1956

his pictures revealed. He was friendly and inquisitive and full of fun. He presumed I was a junior or senior in high school. It took me awhile to tell him I was in 9th grade. When I answered his sarcasm with a little sarcasm of my own, he liked it. He thought I was spunky and I guess he thought I was cute. There was an entourage — besides his dad, there was a large group of friends. There was a risqué poster of Brigitte Bardot on the wall which I found intimidating and finally there was Elvis himself sitting at the piano and singing "Rags to Riches." Before the evening was over, he did a great impersonation of Jerry Lee Lewis. Afterwards, he took me into the kitchen and introduced me to Grandma Minnie Mae who was busy frying up bacon. He wanted to talk. He wanted to know about Fabian and Ricky Nelson. He asked, "Who are the kids listening to back home?" "You," I said. I could see he was nervous about losing his popularity. And I could feel he found it easy to talk to me.

"What kind of music do you like listening to?" he asked.

"I love Mario Lanza."

"You're kidding," he said. "How do you know about Mario Lanza?"

"I love his album *The Student Prince*."

"That's my favorite."

He thought I had the taste of someone older than fourteen.

As he downed five huge bacon-and-mustard sandwiches, he spoke more and more openly. He was lonely. He missed Memphis but, even more, he missed his mother. He was still mourning her death and looking for a connection back to his fans in the States. I found him extremely vulnerable and sweet. He had beautiful manners and an open heart. There was nothing false about him. When Currie said it was time to drive me home, Elvis wanted me to stay longer. I didn't take it as a sexual come-on but merely the request of someone eager for companionship. "I promised her father I'd have her home on time," said Currie. Fog delayed us two hours, and my parents were up waiting. "He's a perfect gentleman," I assured them.

ANN: I was glad Cilla got to meet a famous celebrity. But I was certain this was a one-time encounter. I've never been so wrong about anything in my life.

PRISCILLA: I prayed he'd call me, and he did. I couldn't concentrate on school. Couldn't concentrate on anything or anyone other than Elvis. It wasn't just that he was world-famous and absolutely gorgeous — though that had to be part of it. It was that he spoke to me with such intimacy. He revealed his heart. He expressed a deep loneliness that touched my heart. His emotions poured right out of him. He told me of his family problems — the fact, for example, that he was uncomfortable with his father's dating a woman so soon after Gladys's death.

Romantically, physically, I felt myself melting. His kisses set me on fire, but he would never take advantage. He called me "Little One" and assured me he would never harm me.

ANN: When Elvis kept calling and Priscilla kept going

to see him, we naturally became concerned. My husband insisted, and rightly so, that before she saw him again he himself come to our house to meet us.

PRISCILLA: Elvis came to the house, but not alone. "I'm Elvis Presley," he said to my father, "and this is my father Vernon."

ANN: When we met Elvis that first time, our entire outlook changed. I'd never met such a polite young man. He addressed my husband as "sir" or "captain." He addressed me as "ma'am." He was soft-spoken and sincere. You couldn't help but like him. He treated us with complete respect.

PAUL: I enjoyed speaking with Elvis and was impressed with his manners. Anyone would be. He seemed impressed by my military service and asked a number of intelligent questions about my work. All this was fine. But at a certain point I had to ask him, "Why my daughter? With millions of women throwing themselves at you, why Cilla?" His answer was straightforward. "I feel comfortable talking to her," he said. "She's more mature than her age. And don't worry, I'll take good care of her." I concluded that he was genuine and now I am absolutely certain that I came to the right conclusion.

PRISCILLA: I met Elvis in September, less than a month after arriving in Germany. By the following March he was gone. The minute his military stint was up, he flew home. In those seven months, though, our bond grew incredibly deep. So did my insecurities. It was a crazy turbulent time for all of us.

ANN: I've always wanted my children to have happy normal lives. And even though Elvis won us over and certainly made a good impression, I feared that my daughter would be hurt. I believe any mother would have those same fears.

Priscilla's Christmas gift to Elvis, 1959

PRISCILLA: I visited him night after night after night. We grew closer and closer. Our relationship remained chaste. He'd have it no other way. He wanted his woman "pure," if indeed I was his woman. I was his Little One. He told his guys I had all the qualities he was looking for in a girlfriend. I didn't know what that meant, but I didn't argue. I was falling in love with him. At the same time, though, I was leading two lives — 9th grader by day, Elvis's girl by night. Because Elvis was an incurable night owl, my schedule was insane. It took all I had to keep from sleeping during class. Seeing I was tired, he offered me pills for, as he put it, "extra energy." I later learned it was Benzedrine, given to him by his army sergeant to help him stay alert during all-night guard duty. Elvis told me that back home he had been taking pills to keep him awake during his hectic tours. He was also plagued by insomnia and feared sleepwalking. I accepted the Benzedrine but never took it.

By Christmas, things were complicated. I was his girlfriend. Or was I? What about this Anita back in Memphis? What about all the girls hanging around his place? When one described the geography of his bedroom in detail, I became incensed. He was betraying me. He denied it and, to placate me, he sang such a beautiful version of "Lawdy Miss Clawdy," I fell silent.

He assured me that the gift I gave him — a set of bongos — was the best he'd ever received. Later I learned he had two dozen pairs of bongos in the basement. But when he had me sit next to him at the piano and sang "I'll Be Home for Christmas," when

Priscilla, watching Elvis leave
Germany, 1960

he leaned over and gently kissed me, when he told me I was the one, the only one, when I saw tears in his eyes, nothing in the world mattered but our love. Nothing mattered but him.

The countdown to his departure was hell. We clung to each other. We swore undying fidelity. But what was I to think? What was I to believe? He was going back to America where he was America's biggest star. He was going back to making music and making movies. He was going to appear on the Frank Sinatra television show. Where did all this leave me?

His departure from Germany was international news. I rode with him to the airport. He gave me his combat jacket and sergeant's stripes. "Little One," he said, "these prove you belong to me." He got out of the car, waved to the crowd and boarded the plane.

The photographers found me. I was dubbed the girl he left behind.

ELVIS (*at his Graceland homecoming press conference, answering the question, "How about romance . . . did you leave any hearts in Germany?"*):

Not any special one, no . . .

There was a little girl that I was seeing quite often over there . . . her father was in the Air Force . . . it was no big, no big romance. I mean the stories came out, "The Girl He Left Behind" . . . it wasn't like that . . . I have to be careful when I answer a question like that.

PRISCILLA: At the press conference when Elvis said, "No, there wasn't anyone special," my heart sank. But then when he said, "Yes, there was someone," my heart leaped. He didn't have to say that. Elvis never said anything he didn't want to say. I understood his concern about his public image. I knew how cautious and private he was about acknowledging any sort of romance. So when he said "yes," in spite of his qualifications, I knew he was thinking of me.

ANN: "Forget him, honey," I told Priscilla. "It was a lovely chapter in your life, but it's over. You need to move on with your life. Now you've got to focus on school."

PRISCILLA: I focused on Elvis. Every piece of news about him. Every new record. Every movie. Every scrap of gossip. Germany, school, homework, even eating — none of it seemed to matter. Everything that wasn't Elvis wasn't important. I thought of him during the day and dreamt of him at night.

Elvis, Elvis, Elvis.

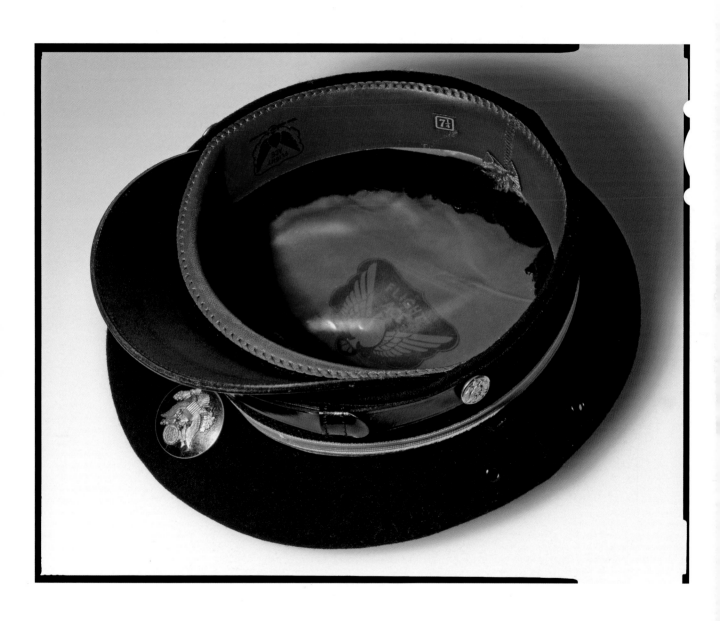

**Army hat, worn on the train from New York to Memphis, March 1960,
and also on Frank Sinatra's "Welcome Home, Elvis" TV special**

Army jacket, Elvis's gift to Priscilla

FREEZE PROOF
TEST
by Rice Stix

U.S. ARMY

3

SPEARRE

Chapter Four

I'LL TAKE GOOD CARE OF YOU

PAUL: It was a tough period for Cilla. I know she felt abandoned, and there was nothing we could do. For long periods of time she heard nothing from the States. And then, out of nowhere, Elvis would call and they'd literally talk all night. I was certain his phone bill was bigger than my monthly paycheck. I also saw that he sent her piles of his records. One in particular was called "Return to Sender." That made me stop and think.

ANN: We just didn't know what was going on. Elvis's career was bigger than ever. He was off in Hollywood making movies. When Priscilla saw him on the big screen kissing his glamorous costars — Juliet Prowse or Barbara Eden or Hope Lange — I'd say, "Cilla, you need to forget him. You can't compete with these women."

PRISCILLA: Every day I waited for the mail. Every night I waited for his phone calls. He wasn't a letter writer but he would send me records as personal messages. Sometimes they were his records and sometimes songs sung by others. The titles said it all: "I'll Take Good Care of You," "Soldier Boy," "It's Now or Never," "Fever." As a singer, his voice sounded stronger than ever. On the phone, his voice reassured me. No, he wasn't going with Nancy Sinatra. Yes, he still loved me. No, he hadn't forgotten me; he hadn't called for the past month because he was making a movie. I thought seeing his films would bring him closer to me. Yet when I watched them — *G.I. Blues* or *Flaming Star* or *Blue Hawaii* — I couldn't help but despair. I was a schoolgirl in Germany. He was a movie star, a flaming star, in Hollywood. What kind of fantasy was I feeding myself?

Two years passed. Two torturous years. Two years during which he maintained unpredictable contact. When I didn't hear from him, I was heartbroken. When I did, I was ecstatic. Finally he said the words I wanted to hear: "I have to see you." He said he was sending me a first-class round-trip ticket to Los Angeles. But what about my parents? How could I ever convince them to let me go?

If I couldn't, Elvis could. When Elvis put his mind to it, when Elvis wanted something with utter passion, Elvis could convince anyone of anything. He spoke to my parents at length, especially my father. He wired a detailed itinerary of where I'd be every minute during the two-week trip. He made assurances of round-the-clock chaperones. And finally, as was usually the case with Elvis, he prevailed.

Los Angeles was fantastic. Bel Air was a land of fairy tale palaces. Elvis lived in an Italian villa. Compared to his plain quarters in Germany, the luxury was overwhelming. "Let me look at you," he said before taking me in his arms. "You're all grown up!" In Germany, his hair was blondish; now it was dyed black. He looked great; he was thin and vibrant; he seemed overjoyed to see me. And although we were in his den surrounded by a crowd of people, we were soon alone in his bedroom.

I was ready.

He wasn't.

He was glad I had saved myself but was still committed to my purity. What could I say? What could I do? I wanted him, I know he wanted me, but, according to him, the time wasn't right. "We'll know when," he said.

Two days later, just like that, we headed for Las Vegas. My first time. A suite at the Sahara. The city laid out at our feet. I hardly had the wardrobe to go with the city. "Let's go shopping," he urged. A half-dozen gowns, matching shoes, all to Elvis's taste. "We'll get you a hair and makeup artist," he said. "Why?" I wondered. "Because this is Vegas. Vegas has a look. You need a look." The look was about super-heavy eyeliner and super-high teased hair. Elvis loved the look.

Matchbook from Las Vegas where Elvis and Priscilla stayed in 1962

Back at the suite, surrounded by his boys, he played me some of his new songs. What did I think? I was flattered that he sought my opinion. So I gave it. I told him I loved his voice, but these songs were slow and not as exciting as the raw rock and roll numbers like "All Shook Up." I preferred the raw rock and roll.

That wasn't what he wanted to hear. He flipped out. He barked, "I didn't ask you what style I should be singing. I just asked about these songs." Then he called me an amateur and stormed out of the room, slamming the door behind him.

Another side of Elvis I never expected.

But if Elvis was sour one moment, he could be super-charming the next. His moods could change erratically, but I do believe his true nature went to kindness and generosity. A variety of pills were his constant companions. They did much to change the emotional weather. I was still learning who he was.

I didn't want to leave, but what choice did I have?

Germany was the last place in the world I wanted to be.

ANN: When Priscilla got back to Germany, she was in disarray. She was wearing a tight black dress and obviously had been crying. Her hair was a mess, her mascara was a mess, her eyeliner was running, her eyes were red. She looked lost and terribly sad.

PAUL: Her eyes looked like two piss holes in the snow. I was concerned. I was worried. I understood it was confusing for Cilla. We were all confused by her friendship with Elvis. Sure it was wonderful to be so close to a celebrity, sure he was a great guy, but how would it all end? My responsibility as a dad was to protect my daughter from being hurt and make sure she continued her education.

PRISCILLA: I couldn't concentrate on school. My mind was on Elvis, who had urged me to spend Christmas with him at Graceland. Finally I'd get to see the home he held so close to his heart! But again, how was I going to convince my parents?

PAUL: I was adamant. The Beaulieus always spend Christmas together as a family. Not even Elvis Presley could change that.

ANN: Priscilla begged me to beg her father. At first I said no, but when I saw how much it meant to her, I finally convinced my husband. It wasn't easy.

PATSY: It was Christmas of 1962. Vernon and his wife Dee picked up Priscilla in New York and escorted her back to Memphis. But Elvis told everyone, "I want to drive her through the gates. I want to see her face when she sees Graceland for the first time."

The first time I saw Priscilla she looked like a little doll. She was exquisite. She was standing in the stairwell and Elvis came out of my grandmother's room. He was so proud of Priscilla. His eyes were filled with love.

PRISCILLA: When we drove through those gates and I saw the Christmas lights and glittering decorations on those long white columns, I felt like I was living inside a dream. Except the dream had come true. I had come home with Elvis.

Cigarette box. Priscilla's Christmas gift to Elvis during her first stay at Graceland, 1962.

PATSY: It was a beautiful Christmas. Elvis was different with Priscilla than with his other girlfriends. Less tense, more relaxed. You got the idea she was his one true love.

PRISCILLA: Elvis's entourage was as much a part of the house as the kitchen. A permanent installation. I saw how he enjoyed the support of his male friends and I was grateful that they treated me so well. At one point he took me by the hand and said, "Someone's waiting to meet you." It was Grandma Minnie Mae. I hadn't seen her since Germany. She hugged me and made me feel welcome. She invited me to sit and chat. There was a lot on her mind — especially Elvis's disregard for his daddy's wife. The more she talked, the more she dipped into her snuff. She was comfortable enough with me not to hide her secret habit. She even let me call her by the nickname Elvis gave her. "Dodger," I said, "I feel like I can confide in you." "You can, young'un," she assured me. "You're family now."

PATSY: That was the Christmas he gave Priscilla a little puppy she called Honey.

PRISCILLA: Elvis also gave me two five-hundred-milligram Placidyls. I was jet-lagged and keyed-up from my trans-Atlantic flight. I hadn't slept in days. "These pills will relax you," he said.

Two days later, Dodger was standing over me, chastising Elvis for over-medicating me.

"Two days!" I said. "I've missed Christmas."

"You haven't missed anything," Elvis assured me. "The fun's just starting."

More and more, I was getting used to Elvis's notion of fun.

Fun meant renting out the Rainbow skating rink for thirty or forty of his closest friends who'd put on killer-diller Roller Derby matches. They'd skate like fiends, playing dangerous games like "The Whip" which might send a less-than-experienced skater flying off the rink. Amazingly, no one was injured. If someone did fall, though, Elvis was the first one there for comfort and aid. It was his party and he took responsibility.

He didn't always take responsibility for his advances to women. I'd get upset. I'd be hurt. His stance was always the same — the best defense is a good offense. He'd accuse *me*; he'd say that I was just jealous; I was inventing things; I was confusing his simple

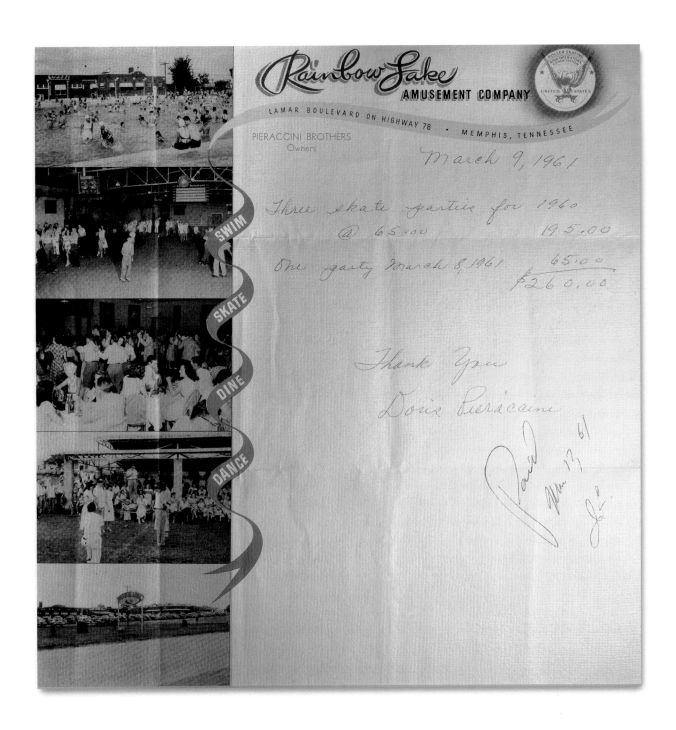

Rainbow Lake
AMUSEMENT COMPANY

LAMAR BOULEVARD ON HIGHWAY 78 • MEMPHIS, TENNESSEE

PIERACCINI BROTHERS
Owners

March 9, 1961

Three skate parties for 1960
@ 65.00   195.00

One party March 8, 1961   65.00
                           $260.00

Thank You
Doris Pieraccini

Paul
Apr 12 61
Jr.

Receipt from the Rainbow Lake roller rink for Elvis's parties

complexity to relate to an enormous range of feelings. Standing between him and a career as serious actor, though, was Colonel Parker. The Colonel was a brilliant promoter, and Elvis knew it. In Elvis's mind, the Colonel had brought the Presleys from crushing poverty to fabulous wealth. While Elvis was in the army for two years, the Colonel worked tirelessly to keep Elvis in the limelight — new songs were released, new stories fed to the press. The Colonel was interested in mainstream mass entertainment, not edgy art. The Colonel had sold Elvis to Hollywood for unprecedented prices. The Colonel was clearly a marketing genius. How could Elvis not be grateful? Elvis would always ask himself the question, Without the Colonel, where would I be? But that question was followed by another: Where am I? And why am I making one silly movie after another?

For all his charm and cocky self-assurance, Elvis was confused. I saw that early on. At one point, though, he was absolutely clear. "You must live with me," he insisted. "You must move to Memphis."

I was still only a seventeen-year-old senior in high school.

"You'll finish your senior year in Memphis," he said.

"My parents will never agree to that."

"I'll talk them into it."

"You can't."

"I have to."

He did.

friendliness with flirting. His accusations were made with such skill that I'd wind up apologizing to him. This pattern prevailed throughout our relationship. Our relationship remained chaste, though we came awfully close to consummation. I was frustrated but Elvis was adamant. Our emotional intimacy, however, continued to deepen. He often spoke to me about his career. Films like *Blue Hawaii* were big hits. Elvis was making bigger and bigger money. But the hits weren't making him happy. He saw his potential as a actor. He loved the rebellious attitude of James Dean and Marlon Brando. He felt — and rightly so — that he had the dramatic sensibility to pull off challenging parts. The talent was there, and so was the sensitivity. God knows Elvis encompassed enough emotional

Chapter Five

IRRESISTIBLE ELVIS

ANN: You hear about people with magnetic personalities. Well, I really didn't understand the meaning of the word until I met Elvis. He had a winning way about him that was truly remarkable. No matter how strongly you might oppose his position, he would charm you over to his side. He didn't do it through force or by being pushy. He did it by being persistent and also, to a large degree, by being sweet.

January 5, '63

Dear Elvis,

Enclosed is the extra ticket your father purchased. I tried to get it to you as soon as possible so that the money can be refunded. I don't know how long it takes, so I hope it's not too late.

Well, I've been talking with my dad and a decision hasn't yet been made. But still, he hasn't said no, so at least I know there's a chance. Like you said, his main concern is living in a strange place and where I will stay. The more I think of it Elvis, the more I wish I would have just stayed there. He wouldn't have done a thing, not a thing. He talked as if he would of, but I know different.

I hope to God his answer will be yes, if it isn't, well you know how it will be. Because believe me, I need you just as much as you need me. As you said it isn't fair for us to be apart. I'll keep on trying though and talk with him and just pray he says yes. I love you so much and don't for one minute ever forget it.

I was just thinking, if my father does say no Elvis we just can't give up. We've got to let him know it means everything to us. He just may say it to test me. But, whatever he may say, I'm ready for it.

Tomorrow, I start school again. With all my heart, I've never dreaded anything so much as that. With no interest in it what so ever. I have to go. I'm forced again.!!

I'll leave for now. You take good care of yourself and remember I'm doing everything possible. There is a chance.

Forever Yours,
Priscilla

PATSY: Elvis had many wonderful character traits, but maybe the strongest was his ability to win over anyone in the world. You just naturally wanted to make him happy. He was irresistible.

PAUL: I was enormously resistant to the idea of Cilla going to live in Memphis. As far as I was concerned, it just was not going to happen.

PRISCILLA: I understood my parents' position. Every day you'd read about Elvis cavorting with one of his gorgeous costars. I tried to tell them that was simply Hollywood gossip, but of course I too had my doubts. My desire to be with him, though, over-whelmed those doubts. I had to get back to Memphis. Once again, Mother was the key. If I could convince her, perhaps she could convince Dad.

ANN: It got to the point where my husband would finally think about it, but not until he discussed it with Elvis himself.

PAUL: Elvis called and spoke to me directly. Always respectful, he laid out his plan. Priscilla would be living with his father and his father's wife Dee. She would not be living at Graceland. Priscilla would attend her final year of high school at an all-girls Catholic institution. Priscilla would be chaperoned every minute of every day. Elvis pledged to care for her with absolute devotion. The intimation was that one day they'd marry.

PRISCILLA: Somehow it happened. Elvis sent two first-class tickets to Los Angeles, where he was filming *Fun in Acapulco*, so that my father could accompany me, first to California and then to Memphis where Dad would meet Vernon and enroll me at the Immaculate Conception parochial school.

Of course I was thrilled. I was finally leaving Germany for good. My future with Elvis, while not altogether certain, offered prospects of happiness and excitement beyond my wildest expectations. When we arrived in Los Angeles that excitement greeted us immediately. We stayed at the Bel Air Sands motel, where Elvis picked us up every day in his white Rolls Royce or solid gold Cadillac. He took us sight-seeing from one end of the sprawling city to the other — the Hollywood hills, Sunset Boulevard, the coast highway. Dad might have been impressed but his focus was on my future. He wanted to discuss my education and living arrangements. Elvis gave him assurances and, even more, convinced my father that his feelings for me were genuine.

While Elvis stayed in L.A. to complete the film, Dad and I flew to Memphis. Everything was in order. Vernon was there to carry out his son's plans. I kissed my father goodbye and thanked him for trusting me and Elvis. It was now out of my hands. My new life had begun.

My feelings were mixed — grateful and glad that Elvis had pulled off this coup; hopeful and deter-mined that our relationship would last; but in the light of the glamorous ladies in his life, I couldn't help but feel insecure. Why had he chosen me?

I wanted to believe in love. And I did. And I do. Elvis and I were — and remained throughout our life — deeply in love with one another. Love has its own power, motivation and strength. Love has its own life.

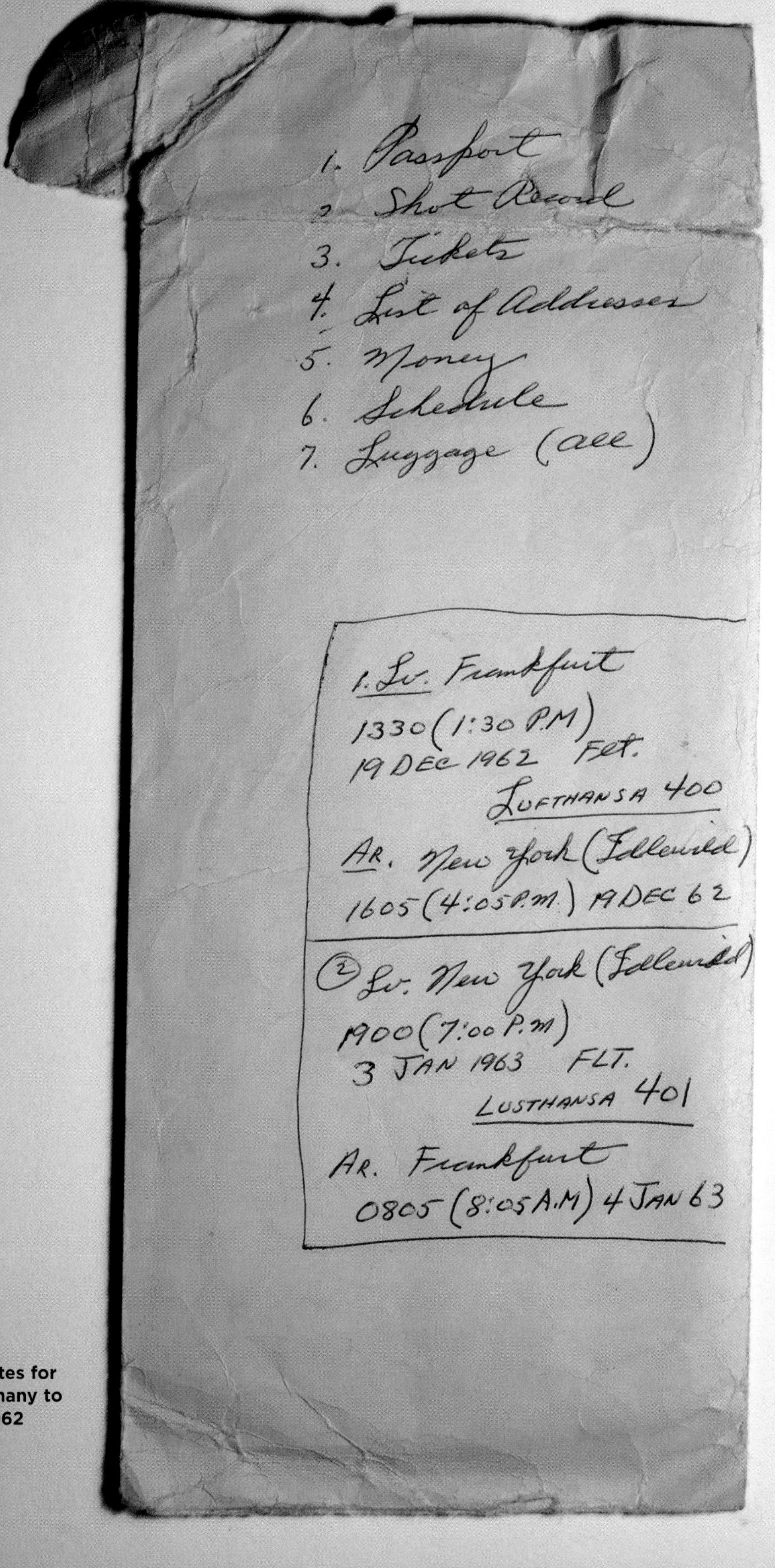

1. Passport
2. Shot Record
3. Tickets
4. List of Addresses
5. Money
6. Schedule
7. Luggage (all)

1. Lv. Frankfurt
1330 (1:30 P.M)
19 DEC 1962   Flt.
          Lufthansa 400

Ar. New York (Idlewild)
1605 (4:05 P.M.) 19 DEC 62

② Lv. New York (Idlewild)
1900 (7:00 P.M)
3 JAN 1963   FLT.
        Lufthansa 401

Ar. Frankfurt
0805 (8:05 A.M) 4 JAN 63

Priscilla's notes for leaving Germany to visit Elvis, 1962

Priscilla comes to Los Angeles, March 1963

Elvis's home in Los Angeles, 1963 (top)
Priscilla, Paul, and Vernon at Vernon's house (middle)
Priscilla and Vernon in front of Graceland (bottom)

And certainly love changed our lives. Love brought us together. But in hindsight I also see that Elvis saw in me a grounded girl, far from the career-crazy actresses he'd met making movies. He liked the fact that my family was "normal" as well, my parents loving and protecting, my father a well-respected and high-ranking Air Force officer. He liked that I had helped my mom raise my younger brothers and sister. He knew we were private people who would protect *his* privacy. He also knew we were extraordinarily loyal, a quality he cherished. Elvis could count on me. He could also mold me.

That notion was important to him — that, as an impressionable girl devoted to his happiness, I could be brought into womanhood under his tutelage. Like a sculptor, he could shape my image and design my demeanor in ways that would bring him delight. His delight was my delight. He felt my desire to please him, my lack of ego, my need to live a life devoted to bringing him pleasure. Our pledge was unsigned, but it was nonetheless clear: He would bring me into his world and keep me in his world as long as I understood that my place was to honor him and satisfy his many needs. I bought that arrangement and, for many years, devoted myself to making it work. As time went by, as my knowledge of him deepened, so did my love. But the world in which he lived — and ruled — was something I never expected. Elvis's world was strange and wonderful, calm and stormy, unpredictable and stimulating.

PATSY: In the early months of 1963, when Priscilla came to Memphis to complete her education, Elvis had already established a pattern — he spent several months in Hollywood to shoot a movie, then he'd

85

come for several months, then it was back to Hollywood for another film. It was a pattern that was hard for him to break.

PRISCILLA: It wasn't long before I moved from Vernon's home to Graceland. The move was natural. I was there all the time anyway. The two people with whom I had the most rapport were Dodger and Patsy. Because Elvis was often gone, and because at school I had no real friends, my connections with his grandmother and cousin were incredibly important. They were both sympathetic people who understood Elvis and my challenge to adjust to his peculiar life.

In fact, it was a double-life, not unlike the double-life I had led after meeting him in Bad Nauheim. I was a prim-and-proper schoolgirl by day and Elvis's girl-friend by night. In some sense, I was also reliving the life of the "Girl He Left Behind," another leftover image from Germany. He too compartmentalized his life. Hollywood was there and Graceland was here and never the two should meet. He did not want me in Hollywood. Of course I wanted to be wherever he was, and so these long separations were sources of strain. For Elvis, the two worlds represented a balance, or perhaps a perpetual imbalance, between his pro-fessional life and his home life. When a movie wrapped, he couldn't wait to leave. Increasingly he viewed his movies as inconsequential. He felt trapped. When he arrived back in Graceland, after being gone for a month or two or three, the place lit up. I lit up. Our life in Memphis was empty without him. And I was willing — even eager — to cater to his every whim. We all were.

I think of the play "Pygmalion." In many ways, Elvis

87

was my Professor Higgins. He relished the role of recreating me. It was another outlet for his powerful artistic instincts. He'd take me shopping and tell me what colors were right for me. (Red and blue, turquoise and green.) He'd like me to wear tight-fitting gold lamé gowns that revealed every curve. In the Sixties, with hairdo's piled high to the sky, Elvis wanted mine piled highest. (Think Marge Simpson.) He wanted my skirts shorter, my eyeliner darker, my makeup thicker, my hair dyed the same jet-black as his. The fact that he was paying this much attention to me was flattering. I was his doll whom he loved to dress. If, on my own, I found something I liked that he didn't, he wouldn't be happy. And though I might argue and complain, ultimately if he wasn't happy I wasn't happy.

I wasn't happy, for example, at school. Keeping Elvis's crazy hours meant daytime fatigue. To help me out, he gave me the prescription pep pills which he had been taking for so long. He even called them "helpers." He himself swallowed them like candy. As his intake increased, I grew worried. But in that area, I lacked the authority to question him. No one could. No one did.

I finally graduated, thank God, fulfilling my promise to my parents. I've never been so relieved. As a present, Elvis gave me a Corvair, my first car. I grew bolder, I believe, by insisting that I accompany him to Hollywood. He was resistant but ultimately saw my unhappiness. For all his self-concern, Elvis wanted to make everyone happy, including his fans and especially those who shared his private life. I had to keep pushing, had to keep imploring, but little by little he opened up his Hollywood life to me. That life, for all the glamour and glitz, was nothing like you might expect.

Elvis's camera

"JAILHOUSE ROCK" - 1957

JAILHOUSE ROCK

Okayed by
Pandro Berman

Director:
Richard Thorpe

From the following
writer:

Guy Trosper

3-15-57

COMPLETE

Chapter Six

"I'M A MOVIE STAR, I'M A SOM' BITCH"

With Ann-Margret

ELVIS: …they sent me to Hollywood to make movies. It was all new to me. I was twenty-one, twenty-two years old. And they yelled, "Action," and I didn't know what do to. I said, "Memphis!" They said, "That's all we can get out of him . . .

PATSY: The first films my cousin made — *Love Me Tender*, *Loving You*, *Jailhouse Rock* and *King Creole* — were done in a hurry, right after his first hit records and before he went into the army. Colonel Parker wanted everyone to see Elvis could be more than a musical idol; he could be a big movie star. Colonel Parker was right. He got Elvis into Hollywood very early. That was the Fifties. When Elvis got out of the army, the same thing happened through most of the Sixties — more and more movies. From around 1961 through 1968, Elvis was starring in something like three movies a year. That meant back and forth from L.A. to Graceland, Graceland to L.A. Make a movie, take a break, make a movie, take a break. In the beginning Elvis was afraid of flying so he or a friend drove a customized Greyhound from California to Tennessee and back. Sometimes I think he was happy to get out of Graceland because he got a little restless, but I know he was always happy to get out of Hollywood where he never felt he belonged.

ELVIS: That's how it works. You get a record and you get on television and they take you to Hollywood to make a picture. But I wasn't ready for that town and they weren't ready for me . . . I did four pictures, so I got real good and used to the movie star bit. Man, I'm sitting in the back of a Cadillac with sunglasses on and my feet propped up saying, "I'm a movie star, I'm a som'bitch . . . hey! hey!" You know, eating hamburgers and drinking Pepsis and . . . totally nuts . . . I was living it up, man.

But then I got drafted, shafted and everything else. So overnight it was all gone. It was like it never happened, like a dream . . . but I was in a rut in Hollywood . . . right in the middle of Hollywood Boulevard there's a big rut.

PRISCILLA: I moved into Elvis's life full-time during the Sixties when he got caught up in this artistic dilemma. I saw it first-hand. Ironically, he was a movie buff. He watched films all the time. Elvis was a serious student of cinema. He loved movies like *The Great Escape* and *The Birdman of Alcatraz*. He watched old classics like *Wuthering Heights* with Laurence Olivier, *Mr. Skeffington* with Bette Davis and *Les Miserables* with Fredric March. He had wonderful taste in film and realized he could do whatever he wanted. He didn't like *Love Me Tender* and called it a rush job, but he liked *King Creole*, which was basically intended for James Dean.

LISA MARIE: My favorite is *Jailhouse Rock*. He was a rebel.

PRISCILLA: His real aim was to make movies in which he didn't sing. He saw singing as a distraction from his acting. If he sang, he felt that he didn't have to act. In Elvis's mind, the singing always reinforced his image as a singer only. When he got back from the army, there didn't seem to be any choice. The Colonel had these films lined up, one after another, each with a requisite number of songs. An even bigger problem was that Elvis didn't like the songs. They didn't speak to his soul or come from his heart. They were superficial songs designed to move the story-line ahead. "I feel like a fool out here," he'd tell me. He felt no one in Hollywood took him seriously and, he returned the favor by ignoring Hollywood.

We lived in several houses in Bel Air, but none afforded the comfort and warmth of Graceland. They were merely luxurious hide-outs that didn't stay hidden for long. Inevitably female fans lined the gates. And some of Elvis's entourage invited some of them in. Many of those guys were married to women back in Memphis. So I became the keeper of secrets. That made me uncomfortable. I was living in a bachelor pad. I saw that, here in Hollywood, casual sex was the norm. This was the culture of promiscuity. I had to wonder what Elvis had done while I'd been waiting for him back in Graceland. Did he have an affair with Ann-Margret? And what about Ursula Andress?

Elvis did not want me on the set. Later, when I became an actress myself, I understood. It's work that requires concentration. Distractions must be avoided. Besides, Elvis often didn't read the script until he was in the car being driven to the studio. Or in his trailer just before being called to the set. He was a quick study, and his photographic memory served him well. Because the vast majority of these roles did not require introspection or even thought, he put in minimal effort, realizing that minimal effort was more than enough.

Elvis had no interest in the Hollywood life. He had a passing acquaintance with hundreds of directors, producers and stars, but not a single friendship of any substance. He didn't trust Hollywood. He didn't especially like Hollywood. We avoided the big parties, the charity balls and fancy restaurants. Our at-home routine seldom varied. I'd be coiffed before he arrived for dinner at six. Dinner was usually the same — meatloaf, mashed potatoes, gravy and peas. After dinner he might watch TV — he liked *Laugh-In* and *The Untouchables* and *The Wild, Wild West*. He also liked watching Johnny Carson's monologue. If he was feeling restless, he might get us all on our motorcycles

Pink feather, promotional gimmick conceived
by the Colonel for Elvis's film, *Tickle Me*, 1965

for a midnight ride. The thunderous noise would rile the neighbors who would often complain, but, not to be stopped, we roared our way through Bel Air down Sunset out to the Pacific Coast Highway up to Malibu, where we'd ride the hills till dawn.

Elvis was bored in Bel Air. The lack of creative challenge in his movies and music made him edgy. This was a man with energy to burn. He looked around for amusement. He bought a chimp and called him Scatter. Scatter was a little scandalous. His penchant was to look up ladies' dresses. The boys loved to watch him in action. They encouraged him. Once Scatter escaped and was finally caught down the street where he doing his peeping-Tom thing on one of the neighbors. Elvis shipped him off to Graceland and built him private quarters out back with air conditioning and heat. Scatter had it made.

PATSY: In March of 1967 Elvis had me and my husband GeeGee come out and live with him in Los Angeles. I could see it was a different situation, much less permanent than Graceland. He tried to fill up those Bel Air houses with family and friends, but you could see he was under stress. He'd always say, "Patsy, I can't wait to get outta here. I gotta get home."

PRISCILLA: Some stars want to meet other stars. Some stars have to hang out with other stars. Not Elvis. I can't remember him once telling the Colonel to arrange a meeting with anyone famous. He saw Hollywood as the home of phonies. He certainly felt out of place, which is why the minute the movie wrapped he was gone.

One memorable evening, the Colonel arranged for Elvis to meet four famous people. But I believe it was the Beatles who were eager to meet Elvis, not the other way around. In fact, when John, Paul, Ringo and George walked in, Elvis was relaxing on the couch, looking at TV without the sound. He barely bothered to get up. Naturally he was curious about the Beatles. He respected them. Mostly he respected the way they had achieved their artistic freedom. He saw how they did whatever they liked to do. He appreciated their songs and especially their film *A Hard Day's Night* where their creativity and sense of fun came through so powerfully. *Help!* was out or just about to be released. He also admired Bob Dylan and appreciated Dylan's serious songwriting. But Elvis, like all iconic entertainers, was conscious of competitors. He understood that generational idols come and go, and that, for this new generation, the Beatles were the new idols. He viewed this whole world of music coming from England — the Beatles and Stones and the Dave Clark Five — with tremendous interest and I suppose some trepidation. He acknowledged their talent and energy — he told me so on many occasions — but he worried about losing popularity. And in 1965, no one was more popular than the Beatles.

The night they arrived at our house on Perugia Way in Bel Air there were nearly as many security men outside as fans. This was definitely treated as a summit. The fact that Elvis greeted them with studied casualness didn't mean he didn't care. He did. He was simply affirming his role as Original King. The Beatles respected that role enormously. When they were escorted into our living room and finally greeted Elvis, all they could do was stare, especially John and Paul. Intimidation was written all over their faces. They couldn't have been more humble. At first it was awkward. They looked to Elvis for an agenda. Clearly

Elvis's autograph, along with other artists, on MGM program

Priscilla and Patsy

Elvis was running the show. But Elvis was simply content to recline on the couch and watch soundless TV. Was this going to be the extent of the evening's activities?

Thirty minutes or so into their visit, Elvis got up, put a song on the stereo, picked up his bass and began playing along with the music. It might have been something by Charlie Rich, I'm not sure, but it broke the ice. Out came the guitars and a jam session was under way. Paul was surprised Elvis played bass. The truth is that Elvis had been teaching himself bass for a while and, given his natural talent, was accomplished within no time. For the rest of the evening there was more music than talk. I don't think Elvis asked the Beatles a single question and I know the Beatles were too overwhelmed to ask a question of Elvis. But they got along and made sweet music together. I regret that no one had a camera or tape recorder to record the historic moment. When it seemed Elvis was ready to retire, the evening came to an end, but not until we all enjoyed several hours of music and idle chatter. John and Paul invited Elvis to their place — they had leased a house in nearby Benedict Canyon — the next night. Clearly they wanted to maintain and extend this relationship. Elvis smiled and said, "We'll see." But I knew he had no intention of returning the visit. Elvis rarely went out in Hollywood, not even for show business royalty. Several of Elvis's boys, though, took up the offer. When they returned they said that John wanted Elvis to know that without him there would be no Beatles. He was their first and best inspiration. Elvis liked hearing that, but even such a compliment wasn't enough to invite them back.

PATSY: The Colonel had a place in Palm Springs. That's how Elvis first learned about the desert. A southern boy, Elvis liked warm climates. Over the years, he'd go to Palm Springs for long weekends as an escape from Hollywood.

PRISCILLA: The Colonel was something. No one had a greater influence on Elvis's career, yet their arrangement supposedly said that the Colonel would deal with business and Elvis would deal with his art. Elvis really didn't want him at the studio — either the movie studio or the music studio. But of course it was the Colonel who had negotiated the deals for the films and records, which meant Elvis's artistic options were limited. I remember when Elvis had to sing "Old MacDonald" in the film *Double Trouble* he stormed out of the session. He was incensed for days. "You mean it's come to this?" he bitterly complained. "Those damn fools got me singing 'Old MacDonald' on the back of a truck with a bunch of animals. Man, it's a joke and the joke's on me."

When Elvis got hot under the collar, when it seemed like Hollywood was coming down on his head, the Colonel whisked us off to Palm Springs. I say "us," although I don't think I was ever a particular favorite of the Colonel's. No steady girlfriend of Elvis's would be. When I first arrived in Memphis, and then in Los Angeles, the Colonel simply tolerated me. Understandably, he was suspicious of anyone who was extremely close to Elvis. When he saw that he had no choice, that Elvis had made me a permanent part of his entourage, he became friendlier and even charming. Like her husband, Mrs. Parker could be charming — that is, if you met her criteria. When Elvis and I first showed up at the Parker home in Palm Springs, I was wearing a mini-skirt and thongs. Poor Mrs. Parker was appalled. She absolutely ignored me. When it was time to visit

them again, I decided to wear the same outfit. I'm not sure whether it was Elvis's rebelliousness rubbing off on my own native rebelliousness, but either way I walked in with the same mini-skirt and thongs. Seeing she wasn't about to change me, Mrs. Parker was more civil. Ultimately we came to like one another and even shared evenings playing Yahtzee.

For the Colonel's part, he used Palm Springs to lure information out of some of Elvis's boys. He'd ask them to drive him down there and during the trip he'd pepper them with questions. He wanted to know the state of Elvis's mind. Was he concentrating on his current movie? Was he ready to record? The Colonel worried that Elvis was distracted and bored. He was right to worry but unfortunately, for all his business acumen and big money deals, he failed to see how the artistic side of Elvis's character was starving to death.

All Shook Up

Words and Music by
OTIS BLACKWELL
and ELVIS PRESLEY

Medium Shuffle Rhythm

A-well-a, bless my soul, What's wrong with me?__ I'm itch-ing like a man__ on a

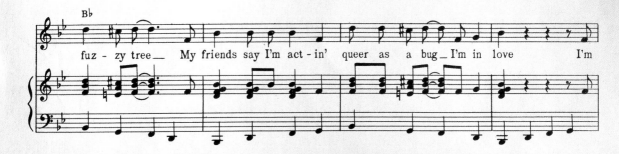

fuz-zy tree__ My friends say I'm act-in' queer as a bug__ I'm in love   I'm

ALL SHOOK UP! Mm__ mm   oh,   oh,   yeah,__ yeah!_____   My

Pant leg from costume in *Charro!* 1968 (left)
Shirt and vest from *Charro!*

LEAVES
OF
MORYA'S
GARDEN

1925

Chapter Seven

THE SEEKER

LISA MARIE: My father's library of spiritual books is amazing. I've gone through those books. They're covered with his notes. He wrote on the top of the page, on the bottom of the page, in the margins — everywhere. You can hear him thinking when you read those notes. He was open to new ideas.

PATSY: Elvis was raised Christian. His early days in the church with his mom and dad were always part of his faith. That was the basis of his faith. Ours was a family of believers. Being an intelligent and curious individual, Elvis explored other beliefs. He had a thirst to know. And he had a gift for understanding different ways of looking at God. But I don't think for a minute that Elvis ever doubted God. God was part of his being. He knew God was responsible for his talent. I think Elvis was looking for ways to pay back the world — and the God who made the world — for all that had been given him. He was filled with gratitude and, even at times when he may have been confused, he always knew he was a blessed man living a blessed life.

PRISCILLA: You probably remember seeing pictures of Elvis wearing a cross as well as a Star of David.

PATSY: He told me that Star of David was for extra protection.

PRISCILLA: Once someone asked Elvis, "Why both? Why a cross *and* a Jewish star?" He answered, "To make you think."

ANN: Elvis always struck me as a man who understood devotion. I know his life took many twists and turns, but when I meet someone with his sense of consideration to others and his beautiful treatment of family and friends, I have to believe that his sweetness is coming from a spiritual source.

PRISCILLA: Elvis was vulnerable and also needy. Given his wild lifestyle, he needed spiritual guidance. That the guidance came from his hairdresser — a man named Larry Geller, who popped on the scene in 1964 — is strange but true. It was as though Larry came from outer space. As he cut Elvis's hair while we were staying in Bel Air, Larry began discussing various books and philosophies of life. That coincided with Elvis's own discontent over his career. Elvis was looking for meaning and Larry seemed to have some answers. Or at least he understood Elvis's questions.

This was Los Angeles, ready to give birth to the Age of Aquarius. The culture was filled with alternative ideas. Larry and his wife symbolized the new culture. They were nice people and different — radically different — from anyone in our group. Larry had an aura about him. He looked a little like Jesus and spoke with quiet confidence. Elvis felt as though Larry knew.

Elvis had been searching long before Larry arrived. In many ways Elvis had been searching his entire life. He had the kind of mind and soul that required constant stimulation and nourishment. Most entertainers with his talent merely accept the talent. Elvis wanted to know why it was given to him; why he was the object of such adulation; why blessings fell upon him; and — perhaps most crucially — why he still couldn't define his ultimate purpose. He was convinced his purpose went well beyond music and movies.

MICHELLE: "I was five years old when I met Elvis and thirteen when he and Priscilla married. Naturally I was nervous. Like most kids I was insecure…" especially around a big star. I remember we watched a movie together — Priscilla, Elvis and I — and the story got me upset. It was *Chastity*, where Cher plays a runaway. Elvis was concerned that the film had affected me so powerfully. He was incredibly sensitive to my reaction. Later he read passages from the Bible. That took me by surprise, but I also found it comforting. He read with beautiful feeling and told Bible stories with great flair and sincerity.

PATSY: Elvis loved to talk about the Bible and discuss it.

PRISCILLA: He'd stand before the roaring fireplace and preach. He'd get up on the table and preach. He'd gather us all around — at Graceland or in Bel Air, in Hawaii or even Las Vegas — and he was Moses with a cane coming down the mountain or John the Baptist greeting the Savior. He was absolutely mesmerizing when he read scripture and acted out the stories. Of course he'd give them his own twist, but that made it even better. It was the gospel according to Elvis, and you couldn't help but hang on every word.

PATSY: One thing about Elvis, he knew his Bible. He also knew he had the gift of making the Bible come alive. That's why he couldn't resist putting on those performances for those of us lucky enough to be living with him. It was always a treat.

PRISCILLA: Elvis worried that he had become a money-making machine. He worried that all his commercial work had injured his spirit. So when Larry started talking about ways to transcend the material world, Elvis was enraptured. He was eager to learn about the metaphysical. At first, Elvis and Larry would be alone in a room for hours on end. Elvis would emerge with an armful of books. Soon he had us reading those books — *The Prophet* by Kahlil Gibran, *Siddhartha* by Hermann Hesse, *The Impersonal Life* by Joseph Benner, *Autobiography of a Yogi* by Paramahansa Yogananda, and *The Initiation of the World* by Vera Stanley Alder.

At the time, we were puzzled by this turn of events. We were hardly prepared and didn't know what to think. I know his boys felt threatened by their boss's preoccupation with esoteric spiritual texts. This wasn't exactly their cup of tea. It was also new for me. For my part, I could go along with Elvis's interests. Most of them, like karate, were action-oriented. But this pursuit was intellectual as well as spiritual. I'm not

LISA MARIE: I loved when he sang "How Great Thou Art." That was my favorite.

It's lonely at the top, and my father reached new heights for artists of his era. He was one of the first to get to this place of total isolation... He was on his own, trying to find his own way. But there was so much crap surrounding him — so many people who didn't get it or just didn't want to get it...

head connected with the symbol of the priest, whereas now this symbol is replaced by the name of a business firm. So men have become spiritually bald!

Let us conclude with a message to the newcomers: There is so much for you to learn in order to acquire the wisdom of calmness and of actions. You must discern masked faces and know how to make My Name the armor of each action.

I will come unto the appointed country, and at that dawn one should not fall asleep. Therefore, learn to be sensitive and to keep about you a radiant garment. And when you are fatigued remember that inaction is unknown to Us. Try to adopt the same customs, and love flowers and sound.

Walk like lions, but guard the little ones, because they will help you to open My doors. Have understanding!

8. When many earthly apparati will have to be destroyed because of their harmfulness, it will then be time to bring humanity nearer by means of a natural apparatus.

An apparatus is a primary step. The true conquest will have been made when the spirit will have replaced all apparatus. For man to be fully equipped without a single machine—is it not a conquest!

The literate in letters can act only upon the surface of the Earth. The literate in spirit can operate beyond all boundaries.

The construction of New World combinations does not flow easily. The discarded centers attempt to obstruct the efforts of the new ones.

We shall withstand the storm and downpour. Our mirror is bright.

9. Sensitive was your feeling that one should gather all courage to attain. There are tiresome and dangerous crossings, which may be endured only by trust in the Guide. He must lead you to the goal and not overstrain your strength. If He should overtax your forces, with what would He replace them?

The lofty mission of women must be performed by the woman. And in the Temple of the Mother of the World should abide the woman.

The manifestation of the Mother of the World will create the unity of women. The task now is to create a spiritually sovereign position for the woman. And the transmission to woman of direct communion with the Highest Forces is necessary as a psychological impetus. Of course, through the new religion will come the necessary respect.

I feel how strained the current is, how strained the atmosphere, but soon the pressure of the stars will be altered. Even the approach of the friendly planet brings difficulty, because its new rays are piercing the new strata of the atmosphere. Certainly, they are

65

In Elvis's dressing room on the set of *Harum Scarum*

sure we understood just how deeply Elvis required new ways of understanding the world. And of course the Colonel was horrified, especially when Elvis mentioned the idea of going into a monastery to gain emotional balance. The Colonel thought it was all bullshit and, most importantly, he worried that it would keep Elvis from churning out money-making movies. The Colonel did all he could to undermine this new quest and, from time to time, received reports from the entourage about his client's new-found passion for sacred learning.

Looking back, I now see that the criticism of Elvis's spiritual interest was based on fear. We were scared we would lose him. Or we were scared he would lose himself. We failed to see that this religious search had been with Elvis since the beginning, way back in Tupelo, Mississippi, when he found comfort in his folks' Assembly of God church. That comfort, of course, took on musical form.

PRISCILLA: I have this picture in my mind: It's a clear sunny afternoon in Los Angeles. Elvis and I are on our motorcycles, roaring through Bel Air, down Sunset Boulevard, over the freeway, past Brentwood into Pacific Palisades. We stop at an idyllic retreat called the Self-Realization Fellowship Lake Shrine. In the distance the ocean is glistening. Elvis takes my hand and gently leads me through the grounds. A sense of peace prevails. Tranquility is everywhere, in the flowers, the garden path, the simple shrines. Elvis tells me that when the leader of Self-Realization, Paramahansa Yogananda, was laid to rest his body didn't deteriorate for three weeks, an indication of his remarkably evolved state. "He was unique," says Elvis, "a holy man from India." For a long time we sit in the meditation garden and focus our attention on our breath. I've never seen Elvis this calm. "It's what we all need," he says. "A break from the craziness."

Because we've both read *Autobiography of a Yogi*, we have some familiarity with the teachings. When a monk comes along named Brother Adolph, Elvis respectfully asks him several probing questions. A kind soul, Brother Adolph responds with great patience. Elvis is deep into the conversation when he hears the name Sri Daya Mata, the woman who assumed leadership after the passing of Yogananda. Elvis wants to know whether it's possible to meet her. Brother Adolph says he'll see.

Some time later we were summoned to another retreat, the one that quartered Sri Daya Mata. The location was exquisite — up Mt. Washington, not far from Hollywood, where a spa and estate had been converted to house the governing body of the Self-Realization Fellowship. Sri Daya Mata, who had spent much time in India, greeted us warmly. Of course she knew who Elvis was, but she wasn't in the least intimidated or star-struck. She was soft-spoken and natural, a person obviously at peace with herself. Elvis took to her immediately. Later he told me that her demeanor and even her physical appearance reminded him of his mother Gladys. We also learned that many of her followers called her "Ma." Thus began an ongoing dialogue between Elvis and Sri Daya Mata that profoundly influenced his life.

Elvis was searching for inner peace. He needed someone to talk to, someone who would understand and not judge the conflicted feelings battling in his mind. Daya Mata was such a person. For all the richness of

Elvis's early religious experience, I believe its emphasis on fire and brimstone was an impediment. Condemnation was not Elvis's style. He was looking for understanding. Daya Mata was the least judgmental person in the world. She stressed that self-judgment did nothing to further our communion with the Great Spirit. Her astute and intuitive way of talking touched Elvis's heart.

At the beginning of this spiritual enterprise, Elvis was wildly enthusiastic. Beyond talking of joining a monastery, he wanted to form a commune. He wanted to devote his life to helping others fulfill themselves through devotional discipline. In fact, he wanted to be a leader of the Self-Realization Fellowship. In this regard, Daya Mata was especially wise.

"This higher level of spirituality," he'd tell her, "is what I've been seeking my whole life. Now that I know where it is and how to achieve it, I want to teach it. I want to teach it to all my fans — to the whole world."

"You must go slow with this process," she advised him. "This evolution isn't instantaneous."

But Elvis, always in a hurry, said, "I want to get there now. I want a crash course. There have to be short cuts."

"There are no short cuts, Elvis. This takes discipline and commitment. To teach others would require your full-time dedication. You have to live this life."

"I want to," Elvis said. "I will."

"You say that now, and I know you mean it. But tomorrow you will wake up and remember that

Hawaii, 1961

you're an entertainer. That's wonderful work. Important work. And in your case, it's doubly important because of the bond between you and your fans. But the work of the entertainer is different than the work of the spiritual teacher. It's neither worse nor better. Simply different. The inner peace you seek can be yours no matter what your work."

Elvis listened. He had enormous respect for this woman. Part of him understood what she was saying. But part of him — the impatient part — wanted another answer. He did want instant evolution. Accustomed to having everything he wanted when he wanted it, it was emotionally difficult for him to see why this would be any different. At the same time, he was able to be completely honest with Daya Mata. She was perhaps the only one who understood the enormity of Elvis's fears. She understood because he told her. The pressure of staying in the limelight, retaining his popularity and pleasing his fans — not to mention placating the manager who helped establish his fame — was gut wrenching.

Christmas gift to Elvis from his entourage, 1964

PRISCILLA: *Why me?* was the question I heard Elvis continually asking himself. Why was I chosen? The wise woman's answer was simple — to entertain. She saw great worth in such work. I'm not sure Elvis did. He wanted more. He wanted a way out of his fears, a life of peace and tranquility that would deliver him from the stress of performance. Ironically, he loved performing. The world saw him as a born performer. But if the wisdom of the ages says that individual ego must die before spiritual evolution is possible, performance does the opposite. Performing before millions of fans — which was Elvis's fate and the story of his remaining years on earth — would excite anyone's ego. How could it not? The world is at your feet; the world is clamoring for more; the world is declaring you King. Who can resist? The more you hear such accolades, the further the monastery fades from sight. Finally, I believe, Elvis sought what could never be his — freedom from a world that worshiped him like a god.

Champagne bottle autographed
to Priscilla's parents from
Mr. and Mrs. Elvis Presley, May 1, 1967

Chapter Eight

FIRE EYES

ANN: Naturally we were overjoyed when Priscilla told us that Elvis had proposed. It was 1966, and by then she had been part of his life for many years.

PAUL: Elvis honored the commitment he made to me when Priscilla left Germany for Memphis. I respected him for that. And still do.

PATSY: We knew from the beginning that Elvis had found his soul mate in Priscilla. Elvis knew it too. It took him awhile to take the plunge, but that was Elvis's way. I couldn't have been happier. Just as Elvis was my brother, Priscilla became my sister.

PRISCILLA: Elvis was a non-conformist. In many ways, though, he was also an old-fashioned gentleman who loved tradition. It happened over the holiday season. Christmas always put Elvis in a good mood, but this year he seemed especially happy. I could hear it in his voice when he knocked on my dressing room door and said we needed to talk. Before I let him in, I jokingly demanded that he state our secret password. "Fire Eyes," he said. Fire Eyes was the name I gave him when he lost his temper and his eyes lit up like flames. Other times his eyes were soft and gentle. His eyes, the windows to his soul, reflected his changing passions. When he opened the door and walked toward me, I could see his eyes were fiery, but it was a fire of joy. He dropped to his knees and handed me a small box. Inside was a magnificent diamond engagement ring.

My heart's desire had been realized. What could I say but yes? We'd lived together for five years. In those years I had learned to love him on an even deeper level. I knew his problems. I saw them first-hand. I worried about the pills he took, I worried about his mood swings, I realized his soul was uneasy, that he was searching for spiritual answers that had eluded him. But none of that stopped the love. The love grew. I very much wanted to be his wife.

Elvis insisted we keep our engagement and wedding plans private, and I understood why. We wanted to avoid a circus. I told my parents but asked them to mention it to no one, not even my siblings. We were afraid they might mention it to their schoolmates. In the end, our privacy *was* protected. My parents have always been wonderful that way.

For all his happiness about our upcoming marriage, Elvis was struggling with the career blues. Making movies made him increasingly miserable. Following his heart, he did record a beautiful gospel album in Nashville, *How Great Thou Art*, which won a Grammy. He liked his new producer Felton Jarvis. But he still hadn't found a way out of the trap of cranking out three films a year. He was looking for diversions, and the one that hit him hardest was horses. The culmination of his love of horses came with the ranch he bought in the rolling hills of Mississippi. One day we were driving through a lovely part of that state when suddenly there it was. Picture postcard perfect: a lake, a barn, a beautiful house, even cattle, 160 acres of paradise. It came at a time when his finances were not great. Elvis's popularity had steeply declined. Even more, Elvis loved spending — on others as much as himself — and at this point more money was going out than coming in. Vernon complained that Elvis couldn't afford it, and Vernon was right. Later we'd learn just how right Vernon was. But for now Elvis and I were convinced the ranch was the key to our happiness. Elvis bought it on borrowed money and christened it the Circle G. G for Graceland.

Our ranch house was small, really only big enough for the two of us. Of course I loved that idea. I'd have Elvis to myself. But Elvis being Elvis wanted to bring

125

down the boys and their families. So everyone got their own trailer plus their own truck. Things soon got out of hand.

PATSY: Elvis spent a fortune on the Circle G. He couldn't buy enough stuff for the ranch. He practically bought out Sears. Elvis loved shopping at Sears. Didn't take long before we realized he was moving the whole operation — lock, stock and barrel — from Memphis to Mississippi. God only knows what it cost. He even got Grandma Minnie her own trailer. She swore she'd never leave Graceland, but, like the rest of us, there she was in a mobile home on the Circle G, right next to Elvis.

PRISCILLA: Elvis loved drama. He loved stirring things up and upping the ante. Things never stayed calm for long. At first I thought the Circle G might be an oasis of tranquility, but Elvis went on a mad tear and, just like that, the relocation and construction project took on mammoth proportions. There were some wonderful weekends, some lovely picnics in the hills, but eventually chaos overwhelmed calmness. When fans discovered the location, our privacy was destroyed. Vernon was yelling that Elvis's finances were destroyed. Right on schedule, the Colonel came through. He showed Elvis a script called *Clambake*. Elvis held his nose but said he'd do it. He had to. He needed money.

So we were back in Hollywood where Elvis was doing exactly what he didn't want to do — making another mindless movie. Elvis got depressed and began gaining weight. Then one morning, much to my horror, he tripped over a cord in the bathroom and suffered a serious fall. The diagnosis scared us: brain concussion. Thank God he would recover quickly, but the incident had huge aftershocks. Elvis was feeling especially vulnerable, and the Colonel knew what to do. The Colonel took over. Enough with these career doubts! Enough with this spiritual searching! Enough with these books on mind control and meditation! Enough with Larry Geller! According to the Colonel, the weirdness had to stop. He wanted the old Elvis back. Part of me felt the same way. Elvis's boys certainly felt that way. Finally the Colonel laid down the law, and Elvis went along. Larry's role was relegated back to hairdresser and hairdresser only. Elvis was now convinced that all those books had only confused him. The books had to go. Together, Elvis and I burned them in a bonfire. They represented the past. Our engagement represented the future. Our hope for happiness was in our plans to marry. And even those plans were handled by the Colonel.

MICHELLE: Talk about excitement! I was told about the wedding at the last minute. Then suddenly it was cloak-and-dagger time.

ANN: Actually I loved the secrecy surrounding the wedding. I'd never been through anything like that. It added to the drama.

PAUL: Rumors were swirling that they were to marry in Palm Springs. That's why we slipped out in the wee small hours and headed to the Aladdin Hotel, where the ceremony took place in a private suite. The chief justice of the Nevada Supreme Court presided. Meanwhile, the press was completely fooled. As an Air Force colonel, I'd been on secret missions. But this was something entirely new to me. Elvis's Colonel pulled it off with great skill. When it came to the press he knew what he was doing.

Check and receipt for Elvis and Priscilla's wedding rings

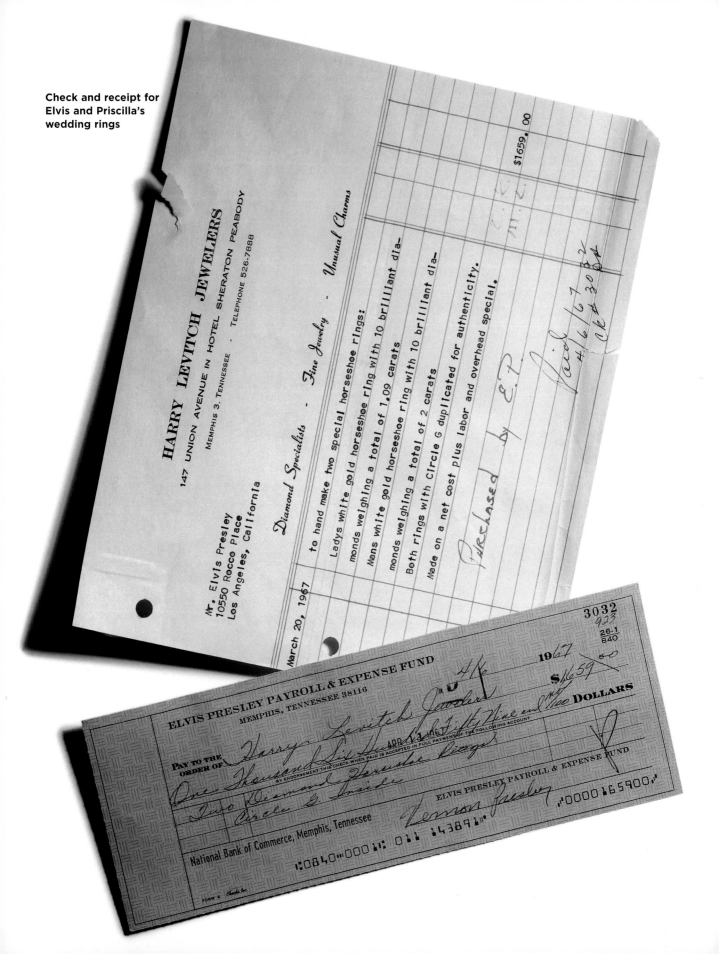

HARRY LEVITCH JEWELERS

147 UNION AVENUE IN HOTEL SHERATON PEABODY

MEMPHIS 3, TENNESSEE · TELEPHONE 526-7888

Diamond Specialists · Fine Jewelry · Unusual Charms

March 20, 1967

Mr. Elvis Presley
10550 Rocco Place
Los Angeles, California

to hand make two special horseshoe rings:

Ladys white gold horseshoe ring with 10 brilliant diamonds weighing a total of 1.09 carats

Mans white gold horseshoe ring with 10 brilliant diamonds weighing a total of 2 carats

Both rings with Circle G duplicated for authenticity.
Made on a net cost plus labor and overhead special.

$1659.00

Purchased by E.P.

Paid 4/6/67 B²
Ck # 3032

3032
923
26-1
840

ELVIS PRESLEY PAYROLL & EXPENSE FUND

MEMPHIS, TENNESSEE 38116

_____ 4/6 _____ 1967

PAY TO THE
ORDER OF _____ Harry Levitch Jewelers _____ $1659 00

One Thousand Six Hundred Fifty Nine and 00/100 _____ DOLLARS

BY ENDORSEMENT THIS CHECK WHEN PAID IS ACCEPTED IN FULL PAYMENT OF THE FOLLOWING ACCOUNT

Two Diamond Horseshoe Rings
Circle G Inside

ELVIS PRESLEY PAYROLL & EXPENSE FUND

Vernon Presley

National Bank of Commerce, Memphis, Tennessee

⑈0840⑈000⑈ 011 143891⑈   "0000165900"

FORM 8 Checks, Inc.

MICHELLE: Just like that, we jumped on a plane and flew to Palm Springs. Then, in the middle of the night, we boarded a private jet and were whisked off to Las Vegas.

MICHELLE: May 1, 1967. It was early morning and we were at the hotel. Everyone was exhilarated from being up all night. The excitement was almost too much to bear. Then just before the ceremony I was told Elvis wanted to see me in his suite. What could he want?

Nervously I walked in. He was sitting there in his tux and bow tie and white carnation. "You're the maid of honor, Michelle," he said, "and I want you to have this." He handed me a small box. Inside was an exquisite blue-and-green ring sprinkled with small diamonds. It was a sweet and thoughtful gesture on his part and something I've never forgotten.

I've never forgotten something else he told me some time later. "It's important that you save yourself for your husband, Michelle. It's important to stay a virgin."

PRISCILLA: Our long delayed sexual consummation did not happen until we returned to Palm Springs. We flew back on Frank Sinatra's jet, the *Christina*.

129

Once home, he carried me over the threshold as he sang "The Hawaiian Wedding Song." He could not have been more romantic, more loving and more passionate. Our endless wait was finally and mercifully over.

What seemed like a new life had begun. We spent our honeymoon at the Circle G. I look back at those weeks as a remarkable lull in the midst of a storm. Elvis was between pictures. I've never seen him so free — free of his entourage, the press, the Colonel, the incessant demands of his career. It was just the two of us in our ranch house. I loved cooking his eggs and frying his bacon. I even loved doing laundry. We shared a new intimacy. After breakfast we'd saddle up and ride our horses through the hills. Sometimes he'd ride alone. I remember one day I happened to look out the window. It was twilight. The sky was

aglow in misty blue and radiant pink. There was Elvis, walking Rising Sun, his Golden Palomino. I saw them as silhouettes against the darkening sky. Elvis was walking slowly. I could practically hear him breathe. His breath was easy, his body relaxed. At that moment I was convinced my husband had finally found peace.

Sadly, the peace was not long lived. Forces he could not avoid — or chose not to avoid — were calling him back. His world would not remain calm. Neither would our marriage, despite the birth of our beautiful daughter. Neither of us could know about the tremendous obstacles ahead. But the future would include more than obstacles. It would include music, absolutely thrilling music, some of the most memorable music Elvis ever created.

Wedding silver and china by Noritake; the pattern is Buckingham

Circle G Ranch

Elvis's gold-plated microphone

Chapter Nine

SOUL MAN

ELVIS: I don't roll my pelvic gyrations. My pelvis has nothing to do with what I do. I just kind of rhythm to the music. I jump around because I enjoy what I do . . .

I've got too much energy and I want to do something with it. Listening to music helps, but singing rhythm and blues really knocks it . . .

Some people say I'm offering a new kind of rhythm. I really don't know about that because my kind of rhythm is as old as music itself . . .

My music? Combination of country and gospel and rhythm and blues . . .

PATSY: I was at Sun Studio for one of those original sessions in the Fifties. Elvis invited my mom and dad and his folks as well. All I can say is that it was fun and exciting.

LISA MARIE: When my father started out, there were prejudices against rock and roll. He was a target of vicious attacks. There had to be pressure on him, a white guy sounding black. He was just doing what he felt. I know he was a hundred percent sincere. People can smell a phony. He was the opposite. He was a true artist and I believe that all true artists are natural rebels. As he got older and explored different styles, he matured. His fans stayed with him because they felt the same thing they felt when he started out — that he was genuine.

PRISCILLA: The energy you see when Elvis performed was the same energy he had off stage. He couldn't sit still. If he had a conversation with you, his foot would be wiggling. His body language was like his musical language, rhythmic, pulsating, always moving. This style wasn't anything he dreamt up to draw attention to himself. It was merely Elvis, a man in perpetual motion.

If you go back to the roots and look at the genre that first inspired him — gospel music — you'll see the same kind of movement. When he started out people said he was sexy. And he was. But underneath the sexual component was a spiritual component. He was excited about the gift God gave him. Like people dancing in the aisles of a holy roller church, Elvis responded to a spirit that came from on high.

PATSY: When it came to music, Elvis had no prejudices. He loved it all and listened to it all. From opera to hillbilly, he appreciated any music with heart and soul.

PRISCILLA: His taste was broad, and so was his knowledge. I remember, for example, Elvis going crazy over an album by the French actor Charles Boyer. Rather than sing, Boyer talked the songs. The tone and timbre of Boyer's voice captivated Elvis. He listened to that record over and over. He must have bought a dozen copies to give to friends. When we visited my parents who were then living in Monterey, California, he had them sit down and listen to the entire album with him. The stories, especially one about a woman in a coma, fired Elvis's imagination. He became obsessed with Charles Boyer's voice.

Of course he loved many voices — Billy Eckstine, Dean Martin, Hank Williams, Roy Hamilton, Roy Orbison, Robert Merrill, Arthur Prysock, Brook Benton, just to name a few. Music was never a mere interest but always an obsession. Many times when he was in Hollywood and I was in Graceland, he'd call to play me songs over the telephone. When he couldn't say what he felt, the songs said it for him. And just as he was troubled by the movies he made, he also felt that many of the songs confected for those films were throwaways.

As the Sixties wound down, though, everything changed. Elvis was near the end of his movie commitments. By then, his box office had sharply declined. Elvis cared but he didn't care. He was more than ready — he was eager — to tell Hollywood goodbye. At the same time, it had been many years since he'd given a concert or played in front of an audience.

PATSY: It was the summer of 1968 when he started taping the TV show that became one of the highlights of his career. They called it a comeback — and I suppose it was — but I saw it as a renewal. He went out there and did the same thing he had done back in the Fifties — shocked the world with his talent.

PRISCILLA: The director of the show, Steve Binder, was young and open to fresh ideas. Elvis was relieved that he didn't have to work with some stodgy old-school show business type. Steve wanted to bring back the real Elvis. He encouraged Elvis to work with his long-time musical soul mates — guys like Scotty Moore and D.J. Fontana — and to recharge the material that had made him famous. Elvis loved the concept. For months beforehand he worked to get back in shape. He trimmed down and, seeing this opportunity to reconnect with his fans, he gave it his all. The set was a simple boxing ring — a brilliant idea — with Elvis singing like he hadn't sung in years. The champ was fighting to regain his title. He wore a tight black leather suit that showed off his physique. "I feel a little silly in this thing," he said to me. "You look terrific," I said. "You've never looked better."

The show aired in December. As we watched it, and as I watched Elvis watching himself, I sensed his nervousness. He was strangely quiet. By the time it was over, though, the phone was ringing off the wall. Clearly it was one of the great moments of his professional life. The barrier of mediocrity built up by so many forgettable movies had been smashed. He had reconnected with his essential genius. He had reconnected with his fans. The power of his performance, the beauty of his voice, the excitement of his body language, the passion of his musical storytelling all came rushing back. It wasn't just the old songs — "Heartbreak Hotel" or "Hound Dog" or "All Shook Up" — that got everyone so excited, it was new material as well. A new song, "If I Can Dream," became his first smash hit in years.

PATSY: The TV special reminded everyone why we loved Elvis in the first place. It also reminded him that, first and foremost, he was a performer. Performing was his gift.

PRISCILLA: The TV special changed the course of his career. It gave him a new career that, in some sense, was an even bigger version of his original career — a man who went from town to town singing songs. It also gave Elvis a shot of self-esteem he sorely needed. He'd been down on himself for so long that even he didn't understand how much a massive dose of success would mean. It's also important that the success came in doing what he loved best. At age thirty-four, he'd been given fresh creative life.

PATSY: Not long after the show Elvis started recording in Memphis, something he hadn't done in God knows how long. Working at a studio so close to home did even more to put him back in touch with his true heart. He loved cutting songs in Memphis. Talk about down-home!

PRISCILLA: American Sound Studios was red-hot. Elvis could leave Graceland on his motorcycle and be there in five minutes. Elvis's producer Felton Jarvis partnered with the studio owner, Chips Moman, another great producer with a long string of hits. This was the Golden Age of Soul, a time when Aretha Franklin was soaring up the charts. Much of this new soul music was recorded in Memphis — at American Sound — so it only made sense Elvis would work there. Naturally Elvis loved soul music — Elvis was soul music — and he loved the supercharged spontaneity of the young musicians hired by Felton and Chips. I've never seen Elvis happier in the studio. He'd returned to his roots, both geographic and musical. Memphis is where it began and Memphis was where it continued.

Elvis's 1956 Gibson J200 acoustic guitar

An American Sound Studios
session, 1969

LISA MARIE: The hits my father cut like "In the Ghetto" and "Suspicious Minds" are great. You can hear the excitement in his voice.

Elvis's guitar strap, 1970

Rehearsing in Las Vegas before a month-long
engagement at the International, 1970

PRISCILLA: In its day, "In the Ghetto" was a pretty risky song for Elvis. It made a statement and certainly had a message. The Colonel was against it. He thought it was so risky and identified Elvis too closely with black America. He came close to talking Elvis out of releasing it. Fortunately, Elvis knew a good song when he heard one. Besides, he liked the message. Finally he followed the prompts of his heart and overruled the Colonel. Thank God.

One thing I noticed when I watched Elvis record — first in Nashville, and then in Memphis — was that, for all practical purposes, he was his own producer. I don't mean that the official producers didn't introduce him to material and musicians. They certainly did. But once in the studio, Elvis was very much in charge. He knew exactly what he wanted and how to get it. He would lead the singers, the rhythm section, even the horn players. He had extraordinary ears and his long experience had taught him all the subtleties of the studio. Once he left the studio, he assumed the final mix would be the one he approved. When that wasn't the case, he'd turn into Fire Eyes.

One night, for example, we had just left the Memphian movie theater and were driving back to Graceland. "Suspicious Minds" came on the radio. This is the first time Elvis had heard the released version. He went berserk because the mix was different than the one he had approved. "I know how this thing is supposed to sound," he said, "and this ain't it!" I never knew the outcome, but I do know he gave more than a few people hell for ignoring his direction.

Over the next years, his musical direction changed. That, of course, was influenced by Vegas. His hit TV

special made Vegas possible. In many profound ways, Vegas altered Elvis's life and carried his popularity into new venues attracting new legions of fans.

Looking back, the curve of his career is fascinating. In the Fifties, he zoomed to stardom. But as the Sixties rolled on, as the British Invasion hit and singer-songwriters like Bob Dylan changed the musical landscape, Elvis seemed to fade. A long string of lack-luster movies contributed to that fade. But at the end of the decade, he came roaring back, showing the public that his original soulful sound was more soulful than ever. From then on, he rode the crest of wild popularity. He redefined Vegas. He toured like crazy. And his personal problems, always challenging, somehow got buried under an avalanche of adulation.

144

Gold record, 1969

October 18, 1956

Mr. Elvis Presley
c/o Colonel Tom Parker
P.O. Box 417
Madison, Tennessee

Dear Mr. Presley:

1.   This contract for your personal services is made
between Radio Corporation of America (RCA Victor Record
Division) as the employer and you. We hereby employ you
to render personal services and you agree to render such
services for us for the purpose of recording and making
phonograph records.

2.   Recordings will be made at recording sessions in
our studios, at mutually agreeable times. A minimum of
eight (8) record sides shall be recorded during each year
of the term of this contract, and additional recordings
shall be made at our election. The musical compositions
to be recorded shall be mutually agreed upon between you
and us, and each recording shall be subject to our approval
as satisfactory for manufacture and sale. We shall at all
times have complete control of the services to be rendered
by you under the specifications of this contract.

3.   If, during the term of this contract, the minimum
number of record sides stated above are not made, then
either you or we may elect to extend this contract for a
period not in excess of six (6) months; provided, however,
that if the failure to make said minimum number of record
sides is due to the fault of either party hereto, such
party shall not have such election. Notice of the election
to extend the contract pursuant hereto shall be given the
other party not less than ten (10) days prior to the expiration of the term of this contract. In the event such
election is not exercised by the party entitled to do so

17. Each year during the term of this contract you will make at least ten (10) personal appearance performances, for the purpose of promoting the sale of your recordings, at such time and place as you and we may mutually agree upon, it being expressly understood that the times selected shall not conflict with any of your prior contractual commitments; for which RCA shall pay you at least appropriate Union scale plus necessary expenses.

18. You grant us two (2) successive options to renew this contract for a first period of either two (2) or three (3) years and a second period of three (3) years if the first option has been exercised for a two (2) year period or two (2) years if the first option has been exercised for a three (3) year period upon all the terms and conditions (excepting those in Sections 6 and 7) herein contained. Such renewal periods shall commence at the expiration of the term of this contract, unless it shall have been extended, in which event it shall commence at the latest expiration date of any such extension. Such options may be exercised at any time by written notice mailed to you not later than ninety (90) days prior to the expiration of the term of this contract or any extension thereof, and upon such notice being given, this contract shall be deemed to have been renewed for such additional period.

Very truly Yours,

RADIO CORPORATION OF AMERICA
(RCA Victor Record Division)

ACCEPTED AND AGREED TO:

By H. L. Letts

H. L. LETTS
Vice-President and
Operations Manager

Elvis Presley

Elvis Presley

Colonel Thomas A. Parker

Colonel Thomas A. Parker,
Exclusive Manager of Elvis Presley

Amplifier from Elvis's concerts, circa late 1970's

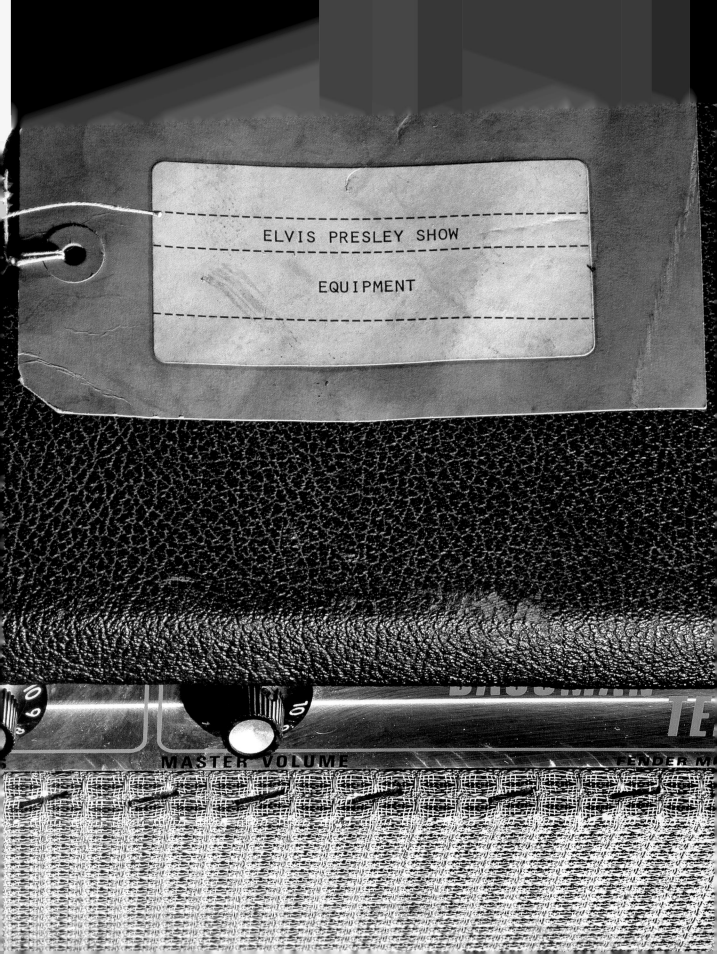

BM	VOID		Time/Date			BREAST	less than **24** hours	less than **12** hours
		BM						
		V						

BABY   *Girl Presley*

Baby								
Infant's Name					Mother's Full Name			
F	2-1-68	5:01 AM / PM						
Sex	Birthdate	Time	Case No.		Rh	Gravida	Case No.	Room No.
6 lbs.	15 ozs.		20 in.		Band 9397			
Weight		Length				Remarks		
Whitington					Turman			
Infant's Doctor					Delivering Doctor			

Chapter Ten

DADDY

ELVIS *(announcing Priscilla's pregnancy in 1967)*: This is the greatest thing that has ever happened to me.

PRISCILLA: I had an active healthy pregnancy. I was determined to keep up with Elvis — snowball fights, hayrides, you name it. It was an exhilarating time but also a strange time for Elvis. Looking back, I wondered whether he was afraid of his public image as a husband and father. I say that because when I was in my seventh month he asked for a trial separation. I was shocked. Far as I knew, we were not experiencing problems of that severity. Pregnancy makes any woman ultra-sensitive and emotional, and I was no exception, but this was totally unexpected. He gave no explanation. He said he just needed time alone. I said fine and stormed out of the room. But he never left, nor asked me to leave, and never mentioned it again. I was relieved, but things were never quite the same after that.

Two months later, on February 1, 1968, my water broke. We were at Graceland and Elvis was still asleep. Elvis was not a morning person, to say the least. He finally awoke and realized the time had come. I found time to do my hair and makeup while he roused the troops. From then on the adventure turns into an episode of "I Love Lucy."

"Where's that box of cigars I bought?" Elvis asks.

No one knows. No one can find them. Elvis won't leave without the cigars.

"Who cares about the cigars?" I ask.

"I do," he says. "I need to pass out cigars at the hospital."

Elvis is moving around the house in slow motion while I'm crossing my legs. He finally finds his cigars, but now he's lulling around the kitchen, getting a bite to eat.

Elvis is acting like we've all the time in the world. When we finally drive past the Graceland gates, paparazzi are following us. Elvis is amused. But at least we're speeding ahead. At some point I ask whether we're headed in the direction of the Baptist hospital.

"We're headed towards the Methodist hospital," says Elvis. "Isn't that where you're having the baby?"

"I'm having the baby in this car if we don't get to the Baptist hospital."

We get to the Baptist hospital, where Lisa Marie is born that afternoon. Elvis is thrilled. She's a perfect little creature, even down to a full head of dark black hair, the color her daddy loves best.

PATSY: I've never seen Elvis that ecstatic. I mean, he was in heaven. He became an extremely conscientious and protective dad. Maybe even over-protective. He adored that child.

MICHELLE: When it came to Lisa Marie, it was unusual for Elvis to even raise his voice. Lisa Marie could try your patience, and one time he raised his voice to her. Lisa started crying and Elvis was horrified at what he had done. His scolding was far more traumatic for him than her.

PRISCILLA: Twice he spanked her on her bottom. Once she colored a velvet couch with crayons and once she ignored his warnings and got too close to the edge of the pool. The spankings were restrained and also warranted. But poor Elvis was a mess afterwards. You would have thought he had committed murder. I've never seen him look so guilty.

Cigars from Elvis's personal collection

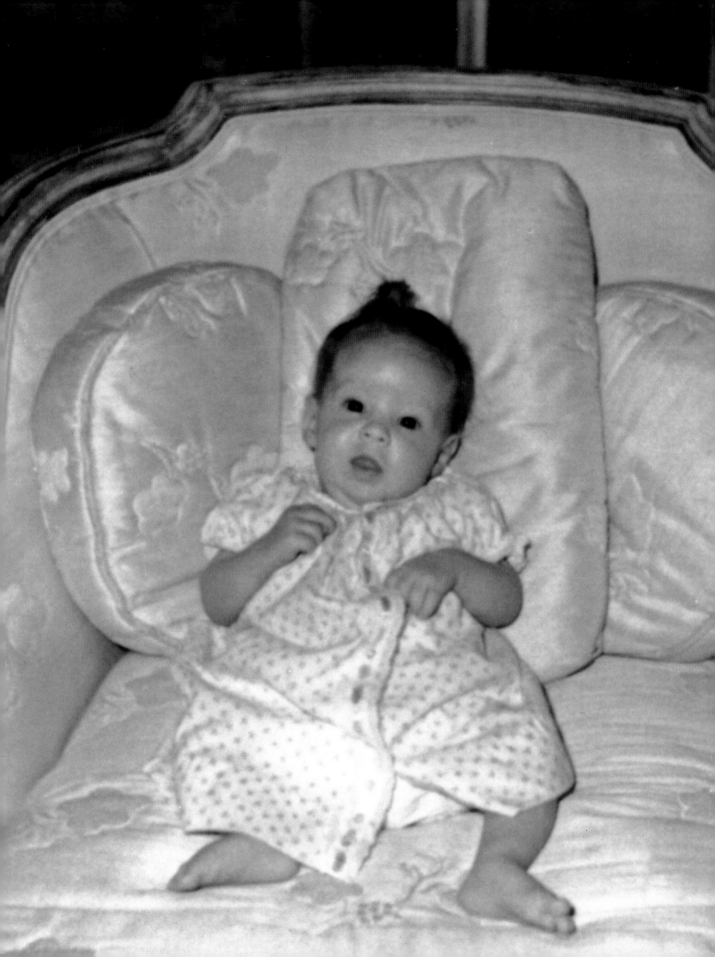

PATSY: I love her like my own, but as a child Lisa Marie was a little devil. I wanted to kill her a couple of times but God helped me not to. I saw her as a little Elvis. She was ornery, outspoken and a natural-born rebel. She'd be screaming and yelling and running through the house with her friends. She was everywhere at once. For a long time we wondered who was running Graceland, Elvis or Lisa.

LISA MARIE: I don't think anyone really had any control over me. They all tried but no one succeeded. My father slept in the mornings which meant I could do whatever I wanted. I remember Pauline the cook once made a chocolate cake with orders not to give me any till after dinner. So I said, "Pauline, you're fired." My father, who was always respectful of the staff, hated this behavior.

I was a holy terror. I'd see the guys in my father's entourage with women on their laps who were not their wives. I'd threaten to fire them or tell their wives if they didn't do whatever I said.

Usually I avoided the front gates of Graceland because there were always thirty or forty fans. But one time I happened to be riding by on my golf cart when a woman yelled out my name. "Lisa Marie, I have money for you!" I stopped long enough for her to make an offer. "I'll give you twenty dollars," she said, "if you take my camera and go take your dad's picture." I grabbed her camera and went back to the house, ran upstairs and opened the door to his bedroom. My father was sleeping. I began to snap the picture when something told me this was the wrong thing to do. I couldn't invade my father's privacy. So I went back out and threw the camera in the bushes. Next day one of the security guards said there was an angry woman at the gates wanting her camera back. "Tough," I said.

Another time my father put me on the back of his motorcycle and raced down the driveway, past the gates, into Elvis Presley Boulevard, screaming, "The brakes are out! The brakes are out! We're all going to die!" Sometimes he'd lead a convoy of golf carts around the grounds. He'd gather up his boys and turn the driveway into the Indianapolis 500. When I got old enough, I'd lead the convoy. That happened when I was seven.

I'd run down to the basement room, the place for mayhem, and go wild, throwing around pool balls and pool cues.

My father was a practical joker. Once he threw a stink bomb into that same basement after locking one of his boys down there. He liked explosions. He liked shooting his gun at a target that hung on the door of a shed housing his supply of fireworks. A misfire would set off the fireworks. Another gunshot once had me running from the jungle room where I was watching "Sesame Street." There was my father sunbathing on a lawn chair, his gun smoking. "Don't worry, baby," he'd say, "a snake crawled out the tree but now it's not going to bother anyone." One night I heard something rattling among my stuffed toys. I called him. He came in with a nightstick, told me to clear out and beat the hell out of whatever was back there.

Another time I was on one of his concert tours. My father and his entourage had the entire top floor of the hotel. Suddenly the lights went out. We heard that someone had pulled the power and was coming up the back steps. Immediately my father grabs me and carries me in his arms. He races into a small room where he sits down — with me on his lap — and closes the door. Then he takes two semi-automatic shotguns, puts one in each hand, and aims them at the door. Fortunately no one came in.

I forget where we were going, but we were on the *Lisa Marie*, his private jet, when the pilot comes on and

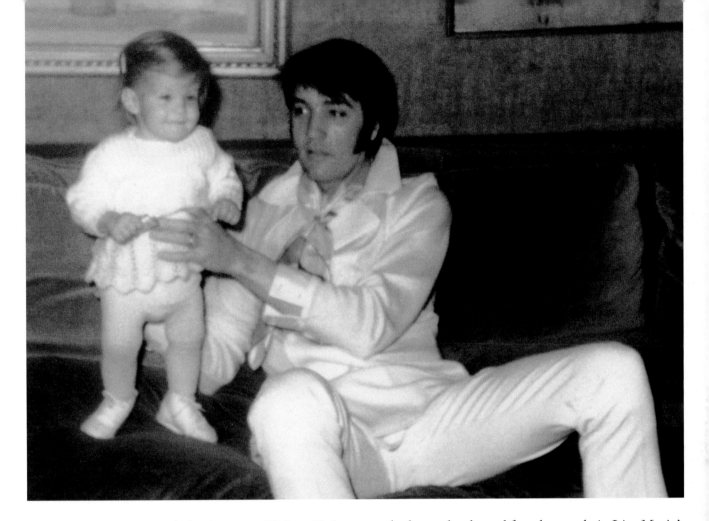

says, "Fasten your seatbelts because Elvis will be landing the plane himself." Everyone's sticking their heads between their knees. The plane starts shaking. And then here comes my father, casually trotting down the aisle, big grin on his face.

His temper was scary. His anger would build slowly. You'd hear a rumbling in his throat, and then this explosion. The times he reprimanded me were devastating. But then in the middle of the night he'd come into my room and, with a puppet in his hand, sing me a song like "Can't Help Falling in Love."

PRISCILLA: The rapport between Lisa Marie and her dad was very special. His love for her was tremendous. I know they connected on a very profound level. It was made deeper by the sad fact that, early in Lisa Marie's life, our marriage began to dissolve. Elvis was determined not to let this dissolution keep him from relating to his daughter. I respected him for that determination. And, much to his credit, he did maintain an ongoing relationship with Lisa Marie. He never ever excluded her from his life. Like all children caught in the storm of parental separation, she had to be confused. I was in Los Angeles living one way, Elvis was in Memphis living another. Early on, Lisa Marie went back and forth between two very different worlds. But his concern and loving care for her was something we all recognized. For the rest of his life, Lisa Marie was an integral part of his story, a story with the dramatic surprises of an epic novel.

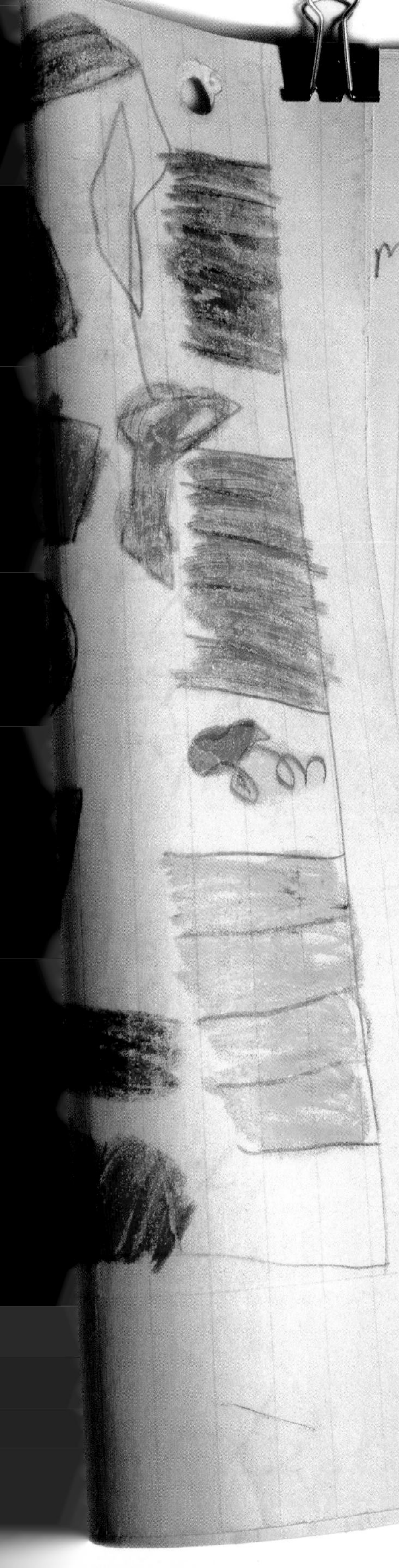

My mommy's
name in Priscilla
My Daddd's
name is
Elvis my
dog's name
is ninja
my mana's
name is
ann
My aut's
name is
Michelle
Beaulieu

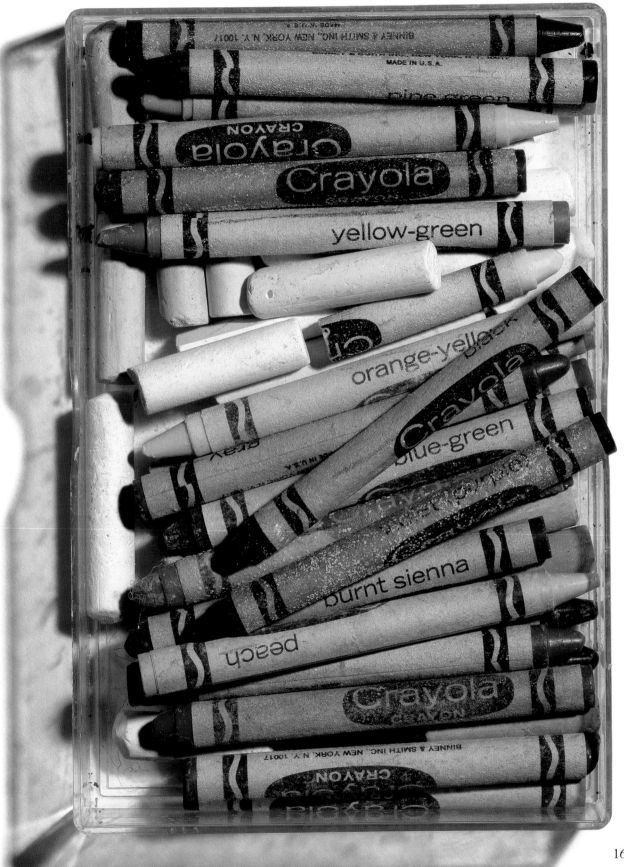

169

FULL BALL BEARING

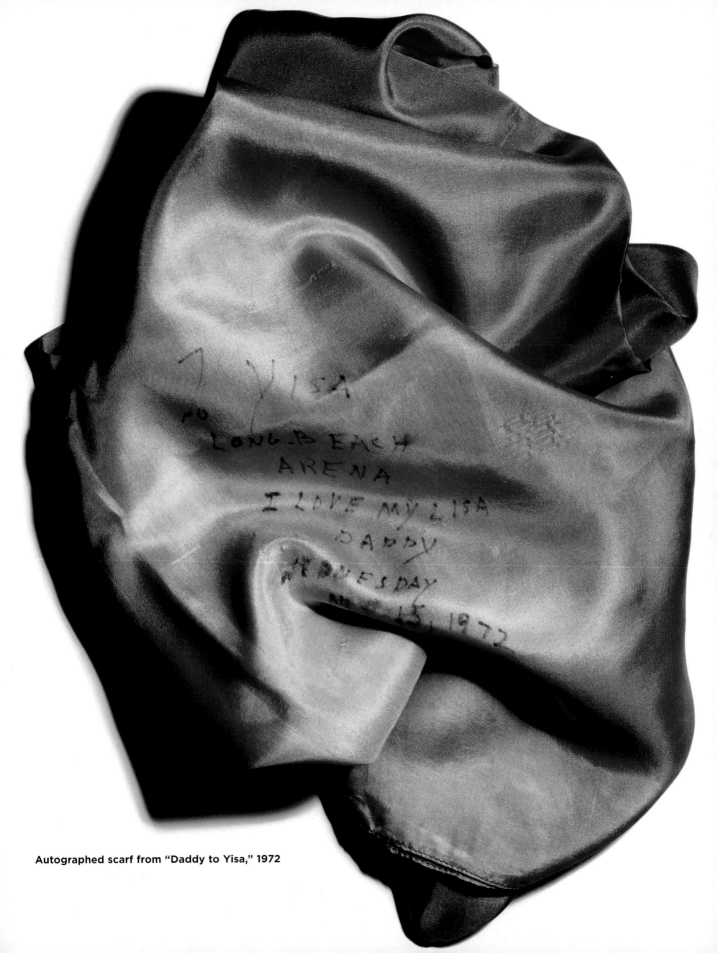

Autographed scarf from "Daddy to Yisa," 1972

I Love

my MOMMY And

DaDDY

And I hope

yo ugis

don't die

Love

Lisa

:) :)

WISCONSIN 1975

I hove

you

Lisa

:) :)

Lisa Marie's personal 45

Elvis's 7th-degree karate belt

Chapter Eleven

THE LAWMAN AND THE ACTION HERO

PRISCILLA: At the start of the Seventies, my story and Elvis's story began moving in different directions. From the moment I met him at age fourteen, I was captivated by his extraordinary world. The excitement was overwhelming for everyone, including Elvis. The enormity of his career and talent was inevitably the agenda of every day. When Lisa Marie was born, though, my agenda shifted. Everything changed. I was a mother with the awesome responsibility of a new life. I was also experiencing changes in my own assessment of myself. In some ways I felt freer than ever before. I began developing my own interests — in dance, for example — and a new sense of self-expression. I was growing and changing. Unexpectedly, the birth of our daughter, which I reasoned would bring my husband and myself closer together, pushed us apart. Elvis avoided intimacy with me. I remembered him telling me some time in the past that he just couldn't have sex with a woman who'd had a child. We fell into a psychological/emotional quagmire that neither of us really understood. I felt shut out. I also knew that his whirlwind lifestyle was not conducive to raising a child. Eventually there would be misunderstandings and mistrust. Paradoxically, our deteriorating relationship would be repaired and even strengthened once we separated. In the meantime, though, I was still a fascinated observer of an incredibly complex man who never ceased to charm, amuse and amaze everyone he encountered.

PATSY: There were so many parts to my cousin's personality. One of the strongest was his competitive streak. Elvis loved to spring into action-sports, games, karate, you name it. He loved to compete and, like all true competitors, he hated to lose.

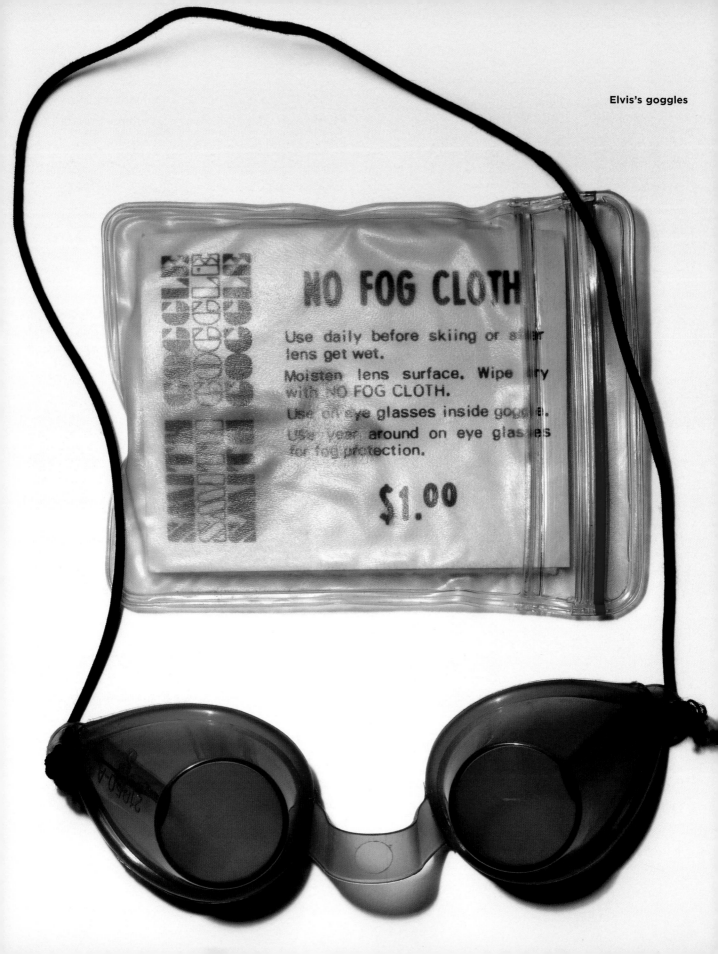

Elvis's goggles

The unwritten rule in the kingdom of Elvis was simple: Let Elvis win. Say we were playing cards and he was losing. Well, he'd kick me under the table with those pointy boots of his, reminding to let him win. He'd kick me so often I'd get bruises.

MICHELLE: We were playing Marco Polo in the pool when Elvis came after me. I was certain that he was going to drown me. After that I became a good swimmer.

PRISCILLA: At games like Yahtzee, if he wasn't winning he'd cheat and accuse you of cheating. Like an impossible little kid. He did it so audaciously you somehow put up with it. You just didn't want to hurt him. You loved him too much to do anything but make him happy.

PATSY: Elvis loved football. Well, some of his boys were really good players. Elvis wasn't bad, but their job was to make him look better than he was. They fixed the game so the boss would score the winning points.

PRISCILLA: He had a sincere and passionate love for karate that began way back in the army. He trained long and hard and eventually became a seventh-degree black belt and an eighth-degree in the PaSaRyu system under the personal tutelage of Master Kang Rhee. Elvis was instrumental in popularizing karate with the American public. He planned a chain of karate schools and dreamt of starring in a series of karate movies. He saw karate as his future.

I also immersed myself in the martial arts and came to share Elvis's fascination with its techniques and philosophy. His karate name was Mr. Tiger and I became Mrs. Tiger. Elvis saw it as a positive outlet.

He had a great understanding and appreciation of karate's inherent beauty.

LISA MARIE: Sometimes he'd show off his karate and demonstrate on me. He liked to lift me by my chin and just hold me there.

PATSY: A part of Elvis's personality was looking for some discipline and order. He didn't always achieve it, but he was always seeking it. He also had great respect for the concept of law and order. He liked seeing himself as a lawman, a protector of the public. He carried guns, one in the boot and one up the sleeve. He loved law enforcement, which is how this business with the badges began. Police in cities he traveled to all over would give him badges. He had many friends in law enforcement.

PRISCILLA: He had a million badges and a blue police light in his car. He liked nothing more than putting that light on his car and pulling people over. He'd walk up to the window, show off his official badges and say, "Son, you were speeding. Just wanna warn you to slow down." The driver would look up, see who was talking to him and remain speechless.

If he happened to see, for instance, two men fighting at some gas station, he'd drive right over there and stop the fight, just like that. His very presence stopped the fight.

Federal narcotics badge given to Elvis by President Nixon

ELVIS (*In a letter to the head of the U.S. Department of Justice, Bureau of Narcotics and Dangerous Drugs, requesting credentials to be an "Agent at Large"*): I would like you to know that I have studied drug abuse, communist psychological brainwashing techniques, etc. for ten years on my own. I want you to know that it is part of my nature, sir, that when I do something there is no middle-of-the-road, it's all the way.

PATSY: Elvis got it in mind that he had to meet President Nixon. He wanted President Nixon to make him a federal agent. Nobody knew he was going until he was gone..."

PRISCILLA: Elvis wanted the ultimate badge from the ultimate law enforcer, the President. He reasoned that the badge would give him the freedom to carry around all the prescription drugs and guns that he wanted. His trip to Washington, though, started out as a mystery. He and his dad had gotten into a argument about the Colonel. Elvis wanted to fire him and Vernon didn't. Frustrated, Elvis stormed out and disappeared for several days. This wasn't like him. We had no idea where he was. Later we learned he'd wound up in Washington. While on the plane he wrote a letter to the President.

ELVIS (*in his letter to Nixon*): I have no concerns or motives other than helping the country out. So I wish not to be given a title or an appointed position. I can and will do more good if I were made a Federal Agent at Large, and I will help out by doing it my way through communication with people of all ages. First and foremost I am an entertainer but all I need is the Federal credentials. I will be here [in Washington] as long as it takes to get the credentials of a Federal Agent.

PRISCILLA: At first they wouldn't let him through. You just don't show up in Washington without a prior appointment and waltz into the President's office. Yet that's exactly what Elvis did.

Somehow it happened. He pulled it off. After being told it was impossible — he could never get the badge, never see Nixon on such short notice — he became even more determined. Nixon might have been President but Elvis was King. The King cut through all the bureaucratic red tape and, within a couple of days, found himself face to face with the commander-in-chief. The famous picture — Elvis in his black cape shaking hands with Nixon — was seen in newspapers throughout the world. The most amazing part, though, was that the President gave him that coveted badge. When Elvis got back to Graceland, it was the first thing he showed us. He was like a little boy on Christmas morn. Plus he had official White House souvenirs for everyone. Everyone was back in Elvis's good graces, even the Colonel.

PATSY: Elvis had grown up on comic books where superheroes arrived just in time to beat up the bad guys and save the day. He liked the idea and he liked protecting those people he could protect. Karate came about in the service. He enjoyed the art and the discipline.

PRISCILLA: Maybe Elvis the federal agent seems a long way from the Elvis who longed to be a guru like Sri Daya Mata. But looking back, I don't think so. Elvis wanted to transcend into another dimension. When it was spirituality, he wanted to be the spiritual leader who could help the most people. When it was law enforcement, his motivation was the same. He couldn't be ordinary. He wasn't ordinary. And just as he had asked Daya Mata for a short cut to self-realization,

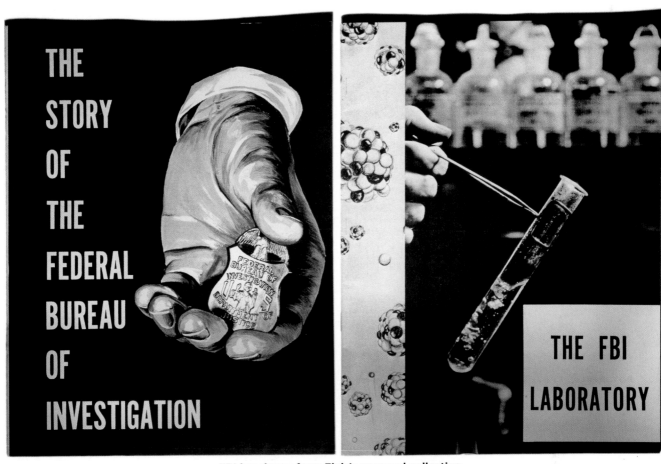

FBI brochures from Elvis's personal collection

he asked the President for a short cut to becoming an agent. Where Daya Mata couldn't accommodate him, Nixon could. And did. But in both cases, no matter how impatient or imperfect his methods, Elvis was looking to operate on a grand scale.

His sense of grandiosity is more than understandable. It seems unavoidable. You could say some people have delusions of grandeur, but with Elvis it was no delusion. Elvis was grand. And as he entered the last great period of his career, his fans confirmed that

fact. He reconnected with his public as never before. In the wake of his brilliant boxing ring TV special, he could pick his spots. He became the biggest-drawing star in the history of Las Vegas. He sold out the Astrodome in Houston. He sold out everywhere. He was back on the road where fans couldn't get enough of him. All the adulation he had enjoyed in the Fifties returned to him in the Seventies — and then some. Meanwhile his personal problems, especially with prescription drugs, were mounting. He knew it, but couldn't quite face it. Maybe none of us could.

Badges worn by gate guards at Graceland

Colt .45 with turquoise handle, Elvis's favorite

**Slot car from Elvis's collection,
circa mid-Sixties**

Slot car parts

DYNAMIC
MODELS INC.
VAN NUYS, CALIFORNIA

1 EA. GUIDE FLAG - COMPLETE
NO. 560 . . . . $0.39 EA.
3/16" Post / Braid, Screws & Ret.

STRETCH
PAK®
PAT PEND

THE WINNER'S CHOICE

Car vi

MODEL RACING EQUIPMENT

#1403 .39 ea.
3/16 Guide Shoe Weight

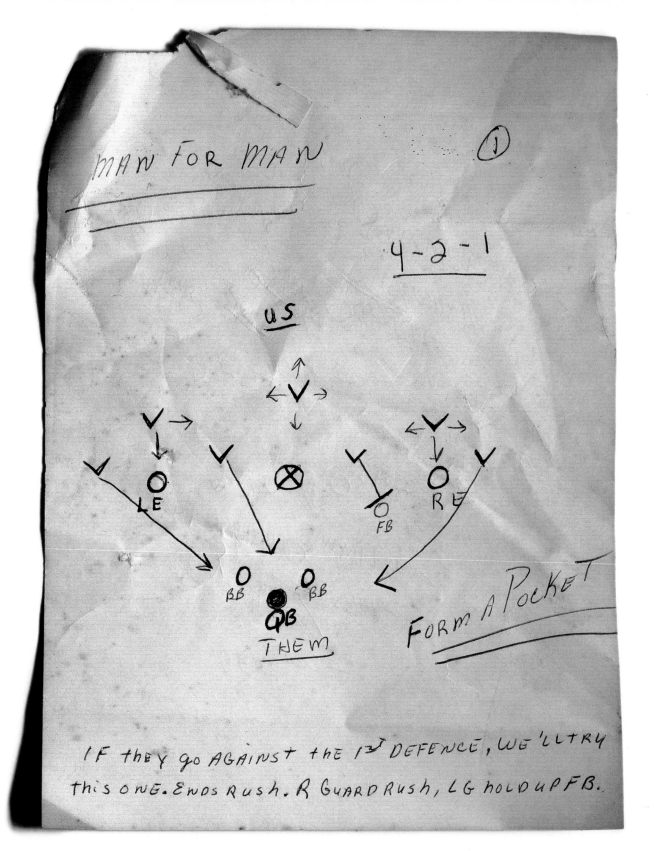

MAN FOR MAN ①

4-2-1

US

LE

FB

RE

O
BB

O
BB

QB

THEM

FORM A POCKET

IF they go AGAINST the 1ST DEFENCE, WE'LL TRY this ONE. ENDS Rush. R GUARD Rush, LG hold up FB.

Handwritten football play by Elvis

Chapter Twelve

INSPIRATIONS

ELVIS *(telling the opening-night audience in Vegas how he imagines a spectator is talking about him)*: "Is that him? He's got his name on his guitar. I thought he was bigger than that, man. Hair flying everywhere. He's got to be a weirdo, man. I'll tell you, stone cold natural freak, man. That's why he ain't been in public for nine years."

PRISCILLA: You could say that Elvis reinvented himself in Las Vegas. He conquered his fears and went back out there, bolder than ever. There was a new look, new repertoire and new energy. The myth of Elvis Presley took on greater proportions. Doing that required the sort of dedication that had first motivated him when he was a kid just starting out in Memphis. Mediocrity was no longer an option. He had to be great. And he was.

LISA MARIE: When I think of my father touring those last years of his life, when he was playing Vegas and stadiums all over the country, I think of the Sweet Inspirations. They were the black female background singers he started using about that time. They brought out his soul.

ELVIS: I call the Sweet Inspirations my analysts. If anything goes wrong I go to their dressing room and I close the door and I confess everything to them.

LISA MARIE: The Sweet Inspirations did an album on their own which, next to my father's records, was my all-time favorite. I memorized every song. They also had a hit song called "Sweet Inspiration." They had sung on many of Aretha Franklin's biggest records. When my father would take me on the road I'd practically live with the Sweet Inspirations. Soon as I got to the show, I ran to their dressing room. They were wonderful women, easy to talk to. I felt like they helped raise me. By then my parents were separated. I was living with my mom in Los Angeles and was not that crazy about going to school. I'd look out the window of the classroom waiting for a car of his to come and pick me up. When the car pulled up that meant my father was yanking me out of school and I was going to see him somewhere on the road.

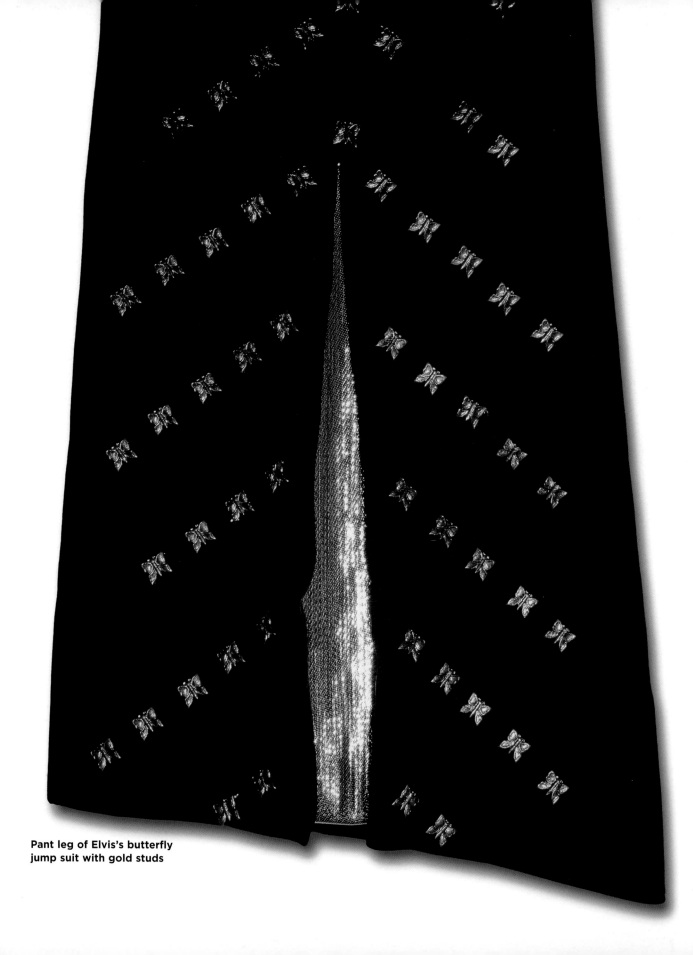

**Pant leg of Elvis's butterfly
jump suit with gold studs**

With Charlie Hodge and father Vernon

PRISCILLA: As Elvis started what became his legendary appearances in Las Vegas, he was in a good place. He made good artistic decisions. And the choices were his own. He started interpreting dramatic numbers like "My Way." He was brave enough to sing difficult songs like "Bridge Over Troubled Water," compositions with great drama and meaning for him. He was relaxed on stage, conversational, intimate with his audience. If he was happy, he'd tell the audience why. If he was sad, he'd do the same. Some of his explanations were long, others brief, but either way he felt comfortable enough with his fans to let them inside his head and his heart. After so many painfully bad movie scripts, he was thrilled to be unscripted and spontaneous. If Elvis saw a guy in the audience yawning, he'd ask him, "Are you bored?" and everyone would howl.

Everyone saw that Elvis, for all his serious talent, knew not to take himself too seriously. He had fun poking fun at himself. He loved singing "Suspicious Minds" and extending the vamp at the end, grooving harder and harder while the audience went crazy. He was seductive, singing songs like "Fever." He broke the Vegas rules by including his gospel music. "How Great Thou Art" was always a highlight. He displayed his knack for picking the right songwriters and the right songs — Tony Joe White's "Polk Salad Annie," Neil Diamond's "Sweet Caroline," Joe South's "Walk a Mile in My Shoes." His voice had strengthened, his range had widened, his soul had deepened. Doing "You've Lost That Loving Feeling," he saw he still had something that, before these spectacular Vegas shows, he thought he'd lost — the ability to move a live audience to tears.

205

PRISCILLA: I was glad when he called for my advice, whether asking me what color to paint the *Lisa Marie* or having me find the huge belt buckle that became his new hallmark. This new Elvis image, at least at the beginning, reinvigorated him. Later, the jumpsuits and capes would get excessive, but for now they established his new identity and helped give him confidence.

PATSY: When Elvis played Las Vegas, everyone was happy. If you talked to the cab drivers or the dealers or the waitresses, they were delirious. "When Elvis is here," they said, "we all make money. We love him." Fans streamed in from all over the world. It was really an inspirational period.

PRISCILLA: This happened in Vegas after we had separated: I was with Lisa Marie, sitting in a booth close to the stage. He rarely dedicated songs, but this time he looked at me and said, "This is for you." Then he broke into "I Can't Stop Loving You." Lisa was a little fidgety so I couldn't keep my eyes entirely on Elvis. Afterwards he got miffed. He said I was paying more attention to Lisa than to him. "I loved the dedication," I said. "I love how you sang it." But Elvis being Elvis wanted not merely some of my attention, but all my attention.

PAUL: After knowing him for all those years, the first time we actually saw Elvis perform was in Las Vegas. I didn't know exactly what to expect, but I was extremely moved by the show. The marital difficulties between him and Cilla didn't stop him from being as gracious as ever. By then we'd known Elvis for well over a decade. I had always liked him because, to be frank, he never tired of listening to my war stories. He had always been more than generous, giving us color televisions and even a new Cadillac. He gave us so much we were embarrassed. In fact, just before my son Don went off to college, Elvis bought him a Mustang. Once on my way to Vietnam — this was around the start of the Tet offensive — he had given me a Colt Python, which I wore on my waist every day of my mission. Another time when he was making the movie *Clambake* I admired a pair of gigantic longhorns that were part of the set. I had graduated from the University of Texas where longhorns are the school symbol. Next thing I know two couriers are approaching my front door carrying a box ten feet long. Elvis had sent me the longhorns. Now in Las Vegas he was introducing Ann and myself to the audience. The last thing I wanted was a spotlight on our table, but Elvis was simply expressing his respect. He sang "My Way," he said, because he knew how much I liked the song.

PRISCILLA: The paradox is that Las Vegas was a place that gave Elvis new life, even as his success in Vegas would ultimately endanger his life by putting him on a treadmill he couldn't get off. Vegas proved to the Colonel that Elvis could make a fortune touring. In love with audiences again, Elvis wanted to tour. Touring not only gave him the nightly thrill of instant feedback and unrestrained adulation, touring let Elvis escape from his problems. Or so he thought. Touring is so demanding that its logistics overwhelm your life. Elvis got swept up in touring. His struggle to sleep, a lifelong dilemma, was gravely exacerbated. His dependence on pills — to chase away his blues or just give him the energy to make it through the day — became more extreme.

Because I was concentrating on my own life and the life of my young daughter, I may have missed some of the warning signs. That is, until the day of our divorce.

Presenting Priscilla's brother Don with a new Mustang

Elvis's American eagle belt buckle

Business   Residence
734-9632   MR. GUY   382-5460

2315 Las Vegas Blvd. So.
Suite #4
Las Vegas, Nevada 89105

May 3, 1973

MR. ELVIS PRESLEY
3764 Elvis Presley Blvd.
Memphis, Tenn. 38116

ATTENTION: Mrs. Patsy Gamble

STATEMENT

Twenty-Five (25) dozen scarves 36" X 36"
    @ $66.00 per dozen: - - - - - - - - - - $1,650.00

       10 dozen white
        3 dozen red
        3 dozen royal blue
        3 dozen yellow
        3 dozen orange
        3 dozen aqua

                 Sales Tax - -   57.75
         Postage and Insurance -   22.25

5/3/73   TOTAL $1,730.00
4/18/73 PREVIOUS TOTAL   760.00 *Paid*

        THANK YOU $2,490.00

                           760.00 Pd.

(Mailed to Mr. James Caughley at Sahara-Tahoe) 1,730.00

Pd. 5-7-73
CR# 12447
Amt. $1,730.00

Alphabetical Index by Manufacturer

1972 *Physician's Desk Reference,* Elvis's personal copy

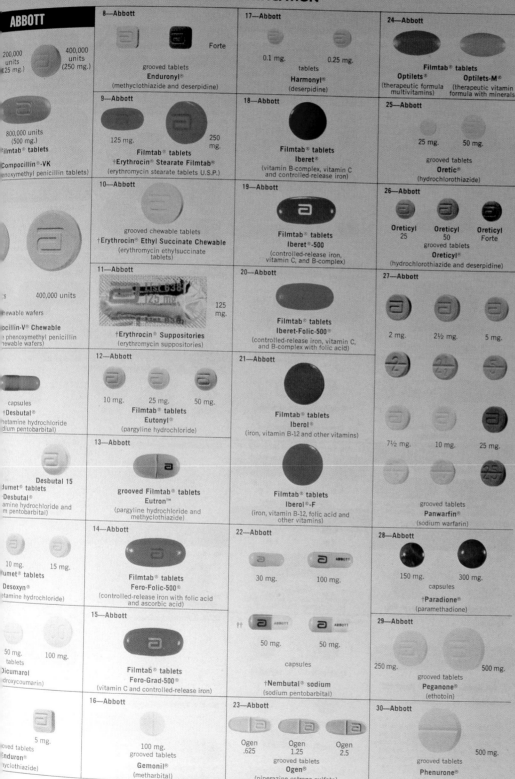

ABBOTT

200,000 units (125 mg.) — 400,000 units (250 mg.)

800,000 units (500 mg.)
Filmtab® tablets
Compocillin®-VK
(phenoxymethyl penicillin tablets)

400,000 units
chewable wafers
Compocillin-V® Chewable
(phenoxymethyl penicillin chewable wafers)

capsules
†Desbutal®
(methamphetamine hydrochloride and sodium pentobarbital)

Desbutal 15
Dumet® tablets
†Desbutal®
(methamphetamine hydrochloride and sodium pentobarbital)

10 mg. — 15 mg.
Dumet® tablets
Desoxyn®
(methamphetamine hydrochloride)

50 mg. — 100 mg.
tablets
Dicumarol
(bishydroxycoumarin)

5 mg.
grooved tablets
Enduron®
(methyclothiazide)

8—Abbott

Forte
grooved tablets
Enduronyl®
(methyclothiazide and deserpidine)

9—Abbott

125 mg. — 250 mg.
Filmtab® tablets
†Erythrocin® Stearate Filmtab®
(erythromycin stearate tablets U.S.P.)

10—Abbott

grooved chewable tablets
†Erythrocin® Ethyl Succinate Chewable
(erythromycin ethylsuccinate tablets)

11—Abbott

125 mg.
†Erythrocin® Suppositories
(erythromycin suppositories)

12—Abbott

10 mg. — 25 mg. — 50 mg.
Filmtab® tablets
Eutonyl®
(pargyline hydrochloride)

13—Abbott

grooved Filmtab® tablets
Eutron™
(pargyline hydrochloride and methyclothiazide)

14—Abbott

Filmtab® tablets
Fero-Folic-500®
(controlled-release iron with folic acid and ascorbic acid)

15—Abbott

Filmtab® tablets
Fero-Grad-500®
(vitamin C and controlled-release iron)

16—Abbott

100 mg.
grooved tablets
Gemonil®
(metharbital)

17—Abbott

0.1 mg. — 0.25 mg.
tablets
Harmonyl®
(deserpidine)

18—Abbott

Filmtab® tablets
Iberet®
(vitamin B-complex, vitamin C and controlled-release iron)

19—Abbott

Filmtab® tablets
Iberet®-500
(controlled-release iron, vitamin C, and B-complex)

20—Abbott

Filmtab® tablets
Iberet-Folic-500®
(controlled-release iron, vitamin C, and B-complex with folic acid)

21—Abbott

Filmtab® tablets
Iberol®
(iron, vitamin B-12 and other vitamins)

Filmtab® tablets
Iberol®-F
(iron, vitamin B-12, folic acid and other vitamins)

22—Abbott

30 mg. — 100 mg.

†† 50 mg. — 50 mg.
capsules
†Nembutal® sodium
(sodium pentobarbital)

23—Abbott

Ogen .625 — Ogen 1.25 — Ogen 2.5
grooved tablets
Ogen®
(piperazine estrone sulfate)

24—Abbott

Filmtab® tablets
Optilets® — Optilets-M®
(therapeutic formula multivitamins) (therapeutic vitamin formula with minerals)

25—Abbott

25 mg. — 50 mg.
grooved tablets
Oretic®
(hydrochlorothiazide)

26—Abbott

Oreticyl 25 — Oreticyl 50 — Oreticyl Forte
grooved tablets
Oreticyl®
(hydrochlorothiazide and deserpidine)

27—Abbott

2 mg. — 2½ mg. — 5 mg.

7½ mg. — 10 mg. — 25 mg.
grooved tablets
Panwarfin®
(sodium warfarin)

28—Abbott

150 mg. — 300 mg.
capsules
†Paradione®
(paramethadione)

29—Abbott

250 mg. — 500 mg.
grooved tablets
Peganone®
(ethotoin)

30—Abbott

500 mg.
grooved tablets
Phenurone®
(phenacemide)

†Other dosage forms available. See description in Product Information (White Section).
††New orange and white capsule to be adopted during 1972.

Chapter Thirteen

ELVIS'S HANDS

ELVIS: Rumors that you hear about me are trash. I'm an eighth-degree black belt in karate. I am a Federal Agent. I am, swear to God. They don't give you that if you're strung out.

PRISCILLA: My sister Michelle accompanied me to Santa Monica, where Elvis and I were officially divorced in October 1973. It was an amazing day. Amazing, I believe, because as we sat in the judge's chambers and signed the final decree, we held hands. It was as though we were an old married couple rather than about-to-be divorced adversaries. There was nothing hostile about it. He was tender and sweet with me. But as Elvis's fingers touched mine, I grew alarmed. His hands, always smooth, were puffy, swollen. I knew something was different; something was wrong. I could see it in his eyes, I could feel it in his hands.

ANN: After their divorce, Elvis wouldn't let go. He called me and said, "Please speak with Cilla." He begged me to convince her to go back to him. It was a very sad conversation. I felt how desperately he wanted to keep his family together, but I also knew Priscilla had made a measured and mature decision to move on with her life. At the same, I assured Elvis I'd do whatever I could. "Please do," he pleaded. "I want you all to be part of my family." "Elvis," I said, "we'll always be part of your family."

Afterwards, my mind was flooded with memories. I remember how Elvis and Cilla had come to our house in Mount Holly, New Jersey, because he wanted to be there when our son Don returned home from Vietnam. He wanted to be part of the joyous celebration. He loved the feeling of family.

PRISCILLA: It might be midnight. It might be 2 a.m. Time didn't matter to him. Elvis was calling, saying he was on his way over. He had a song for me to hear and a new book for me to read. He was deep into numerology and wanted to explain its meaning.

But basically he was lonely and needed company. He needed to reconnect with family. I might complain that he was calling in the middle of the night, but I never refused a visit. I knew what it meant to him.

LISA MARIE: After my parents' separation and divorce, I felt no animosity between them. He was always over the house talking to Mom all hours of the night. He conferred with her about everything.

PRISCILLA: From 1973 on, it was clear that Elvis was hurting more and more. People have asked, "Why didn't you initiate an intervention?" People who ask that don't know Elvis. Elvis would no more have responded to an intervention than a demand to give up singing. It's important to realize that, for two different reasons, he never considered himself a drug addict. First, his drugs were all prescribed. That made a big difference in his mind. And secondly, he hated street drugs and campaigned for their elimination. So how could he be an addict himself? He refused to believe he had a problem. He would have undoubtedly laughed away any attempt at an intervention. There's no one, including his father, who could have pulled that off.

ELVIS (*note written in his Hilton suite in Las Vegas*):
I feel so alone sometimes
The night is quiet for me
I would love to be able to sleep
I'm glad everyone is gone now
I will probably not rest tonight
I have no need for all of this
Help me, Lord

LISA MARIE: When I stayed at Graceland I could see he was struggling. I could feel that he was very sad. He'd come into my room walking so unsteadily that sometimes he'd start to fall and I'd have to catch him. He had his own chair in my bedroom where he'd sit, watch my TV and smoke cigars.

PRISCILLA: In 1975, I got a letter from Sri Daya Mata saying she needed to get in touch with Elvis because she was feeling his distress. When I spoke to her she said she had sent him many letters, all unanswered. From what I understood, Vernon tore them up. He was afraid of Elvis getting re-entangled with a spiritual search that might take him away from touring. I called Elvis and told him that Daya Mata was concerned and wanted to speak with him. He was moved. I know he still regarded her highly, but he never called her.

I saw a ray of hope when Barbra Streisand asked Elvis to costar with her in the remake of *A Star Is Born*. Elvis would have been magnificent in the role. I encouraged him. I thought the movie might give him new life. I know he wanted to do it, but somehow, in the hands of the Colonel, negotiations hit a snag and the part went to Kris Kristofferson. Such a unique opportunity, especially in the area of acting, never came Elvis's way again. He returned to the routine of non-stop performances.

MICHELLE: We saw him perform in Las Vegas in December of 1976. After the show he invited us to his dressing room. He spoke about his hands. He was self-conscious that they were so bloated. I patted his hands, as if to reassure him.

I was excited to introduce him to my boyfriend Gary, who was a big fan. He treated us all like family. Well, we were family. We are family. He treated Mom and Dad like his own mother and father. He had them sitting right next to him in his dressing room for what seemed like hours.

ANN: Elvis loved talking to Paul. He respected him so. Even the Colonel called my husband "the real Colonel."

PAUL: It was very moving. He didn't want to let us go. He kept thinking of topics that would prolong the conversation — his plans to expand his gun collection, his touring schedule, whatever came to mind. He kept asking us what we needed and wanted. We told him that we were just fine. We had everything we needed. But he insisted that we accept something.

ANN: He wrote out a check for $10,000 and handed it to us, saying, "This is to fix up your house."

PAUL: This from an ex-son-in-law.

ANN: The more we stayed and spoke with him, the more worried I became about his health. He was sweet and loving but he was distracted in a way I had never seen before. Something wasn't right. When we finally left, I had this sinking feeling in the pit of my stomach.

ELVIS *(note written in his Hilton suite in Vegas)*: I don't know who I can talk to anymore. Or turn to. I only have myself and the Lord. Help me, Lord, to know the right thing.

LISA MARIE: I don't like talking about this. It was August 16th at four a.m., I was supposed to be asleep actually. And he found me and said, you know, go to bed. And I said, okay, and I think he kissed me goodnight and I ran off. And he had come in and kissed me goodnight after that. That was the last time I saw him alive.

MICHELLE: On August 16, 1977, Priscilla was meeting me for lunch at a restaurant on Melrose Avenue in Los Angeles.

PRISCILLA: I left the house knowing something was wrong.

The air was wrong. The sky was wrong. I had a meeting earlier that morning during which I felt like the world was wrong. Something was putting me on edge. Something grave.

I was late meeting Michelle. When I saw her waiting for me in front of the restaurant, I grew even more alarmed. I could see it in her eyes. "Something's wrong," she said. "Elvis is in the hospital." Elvis had been in the hospital before. After many tours he'd check in to rest and recover from the strain. He had gone through several serious health bouts, but always pulled through. He was still young, only forty-two, and vital. Elvis was strong.

"What is it?" I asked Michelle. "What's wrong?"

"You have to call Memphis."

I ran every red light and nearly ran off the road before reaching my house. Inside I heard the phone ringing. I fumbled with my keys, I screamed inside, I finally got the door opened and raced to the phone. My worst fears were confirmed. He was gone. Elvis was gone.

My first thought was of Lisa Marie.

I called my daughter immediately and told her to stay in Grandma's room. Lisa was hysterical. I could hear Vernon crying and moaning in the distance. The pain in his voice pierced my heart.

I had them send the plane for me.

"I'll be right there, baby," I told Lisa.

"I'll be there in no time."

THE PRAYER KEY
NEW TESTAMENT

ELVIS PRESLEY

Chapter Fourteen

STILL

ELVIS *(note written in his Hilton suite in Las Vegas, quoting the 46th Psalm):* "Be still and know that I am God."

Elvis's guitar case, circa late 1970's

PATSY: I know one thing about my cousin: He loved the Lord and always did the best he could. He tried his hardest. He was a human being and that means he had faults. But his heart was bigger than all of Mississippi and Tennessee combined. And as long as there's some kind of gizmo to listen to music, people are going to be listening to Elvis. And loving him. Because all his love is right there in his music.

PRISCILLA: The last year of his life was rough. I knew that. I knew he was having all sorts of heartache. He wasn't happy. As a result, he abused his body. It was that abuse that killed him. I don't believe there was foul play. It's simply that Elvis thought he was indestructible. We thought the same thing. After all, he was worshiped by a world of fans who treated him like a god. He was misunderstood by those around him, especially at the end. We underestimated his emotional pain. And he lacked the means to fully express that pain.

Memphis Press-Scimitar

SPECIAL EDITION

U.S. WEATHER FORECAST: A 60 per cent chance of rain with high in the upper 80s. Low tonight low 70s. High Thursday mid 80s.

97TH YEAR | MEMPHIS, TENN., WEDNESDAY, AUGUST 17, 1977 | TELEPHONES: NEWS and GENERAL 526-2141 / CIRCULATION 525-7801 / WANT ADS 526-0092

Memphis Leads the World in Mourning the Monarch of Rock 'n Roll

A Lonely Life Ends on Elvis Presley Boulevard

By CLARK PORTEOUS
Press-Scimitar Staff Writer

(Aug. 17,1977)

The King is dead.

Elvis Presley — the jiggling, jiving, rock 'n roll king — lived just 42 years, seven months and eight days.

It was an exciting but frustrating life which ended in Baptist Hospital, where Elvis was pronounced dead at 3:30 p.m. yesterday of a heart attack.

Elvis made millions of dollars and literally was worshipped by millions of fans. But he was lonesome much of the time, paid a high price for privacy and could not do many things he would have liked to do because he always drew a crowd of admirers.

Elvis, with a pleasant singing voice and a new style, strumming a guitar and gyrating his pelvis — which brought him the name in early days of "Elvis the Pelvis" — made millions, was able to buy anything he wanted, yet happiness seemed to elude him.

Elvis gave away countless thousands, giving funds to numerous Memphis institutions just before Christmas every year. He would give his friends — and occasionally even strangers — expensive automobiles.

Yet as the years passed, many of his friends seemed to have faded away, not generally because they wanted to, but some said Elvis had changed.

Elvis Aron Presley was written about on his 40th birthday, and friends were quoted as saying he was "fat and forty" and refused to see anybody until his weight got down to his regular trim 180 pounds. He was staying in his mansion, Graceland, on Elvis Presley Boulevard, a part of Bellevue renamed by city fathers to honor Elvis.

He became more and more of a recluse in his last few years. Red West and other close friends, who used to be called the "Memphis Mafia," were no longer with him.

Elvis, already a living legend and somewhat of a folk hero to many, was found unconscious at Graceland at 2:30 p.m. yesterday.

Maurice Elliott, Baptist Hospital vice president, said Joe Esposito, Presley's road manager and long-time friend, called an ambulance and tried to revive Elvis with mouth-to-mouth resuscitation and heart massage until the ambulance arrived. Efforts to revive Presley continued

---

A Tribute to Elvis

The unexpected death of rock 'n roll star Elvis Presley Aug. 16, 1977, was news of international impact. Almost every news agency in the world reported the tragedy under a Memphis dateline.

The public interest required that many members of *The Press-Scimitar* staff have a hand in compiling and presenting the story. Every conceivable angle was covered in a period of five publication days. Requests for copies of *The Press-Scimitar* containing coverage of the singer's death poured in from all over the world in great numbers. It was impossible to meet the demand.

Therefore, as a public service to its readers, *The Press-Scimitar* has reprinted in this special tribute edition all Elvis Presley stories and pictures published in the five-day period. With as few changes as possible, all stories and pictures that we published in the regular editions of *The Press-Scimitar* are reprinted herein. This edition plus a similar edition of *The Commercial Appeal* are offered to readers for 50 cents.

"**Goodby, darling, goodby** — I loved you so much," a sobbing Elvis said before leaving the burial site. "I lived my whole life just for you."

Elvis once recalled that in his boyhood his mother was very possessive of him, probably due to the loss of the twin. The Presleys had no other children.

"My mama never let me out of her sight," Elvis said. "I couldn't go down to the creek with the other kids. Sometimes, when I was little, I used to run off. Mama would whip me and I thought she didn't love me."

Elvis knew extreme poverty as well as extreme wealth.

His father, Vernon, who has shared in his son's success, did odd jobs and farmed in Tupelo, but the family was poor. When Elvis was 14, the family moved to Memphis. They Lived in a one-room apartment on Alabama in North Memphis at first, later moved into Lauderdale Courts, one of the two first public housing projects built in Memphis in the mid-'30s.

Elvis went to Humes High, where he

Elvis was graduated from Humes in 1953. He had been too small to make the football team, but he was interested in sports and learned to be an expert at karate.

After graduation from Humes, Elvis worked on the assembly line of a precision tool company, then at a furniture factory making plastic tables and then as a truck driver for Crown Electric Co. He also ushered at Loew's State, a theater which was later to show many of his movies.

In the summer of 1953, Elvis took the step which led to fame and fortune. He had "just an urgin'" and went to Sam Phillips' Sun Record Co. He paid to have a recording made for his mother. Elvis said "it sounded like somebody beating on a bucket lid." But Elvis was told he had an unusual voice and someone might call him.

Months passed and Elvis kept driving a truck for $35 a week. At night he attended a trade school, studying to be an electrician.

Then in the spring of 1954, lightning struck and Phillips called Elvis and asked

ELVIS PRESLEY: THE BEAT WENT ON — AND ON AND ON

— UPI Telephoto

Mourners In Waiting For Last Homecoming Of Revered Singer

By CHARLES GOODMAN and HENRY BAILEY
Press-Scimitar Staff Writers

(Aug. 17, 1977)

the crowd, which had surged forward. A hearse entered behind police motorcycles, and the crowd watched as a copper casket was carried up the steps of Graceland and

— Staff Photo by William L. Leaptrott
MOURNER AT GRACELAND

229

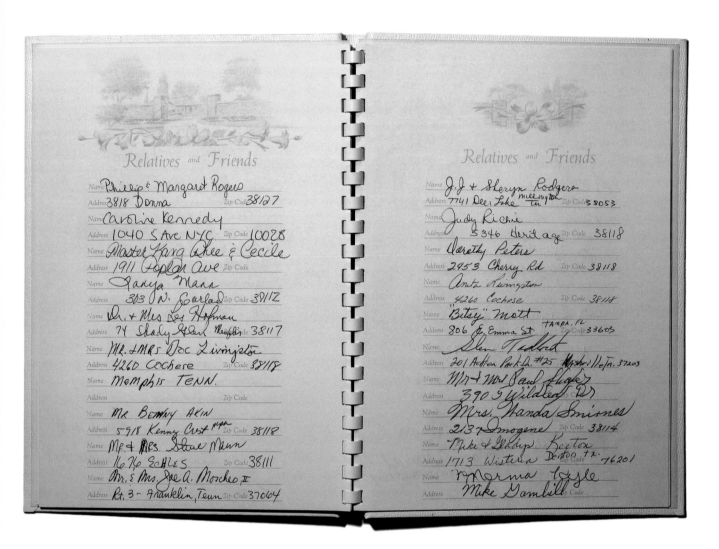

Relatives and Friends

Name Phillip & Margaret Rogers
Address 3818 Donna   Zip Code 38127
Name Caroline Kennedy
Address 1040 5 Ave NYC   Zip Code 10028
Name Master Kang Ahee & Cecile
Address 1911 Poplar Ave   Zip Code
Name Kanya Mann
Address 303 N. Goarland   Zip Code 38112
Name Dr. & Mrs Les Hofman
Address 74 Shady Glen Memphis Zip Code 38117
Name Mr. & Mrs Doc Livingston
Address 4260 Cochere   Zip Code 38118
Name Memphis TENN.
Address   Zip Code
Name Mr Benny Akin
Address 5918 Kenny Crest Mem Zip Code 38118
Name Mr. & Mrs. Steve Mann
Address 1676 Echles   Zip Code 38111
Name Mr. & Mrs. Joe A. Monchez II
Address Rt. 3 - Franklin, Tenn Zip Code 37064

Relatives and Friends

Name J. J. & Sheryn Rodgers
Address 7741 Deer Lake Millington Tn Zip Code 38053
Name Judy Richie
Address 5346 Heritage   Zip Code 38118
Name Dorothy Peters
Address 2953 Cherry Rd   Zip Code 38118
Name Anita Livingston
Address 4260 Cochese   Zip Code 38118
Name "Betsy" Mott
Address 806 E. Emma St Tampa, FL Zip Code 33603
Name Glen Tidbet
Address 201 Action Park D. #25 Nashville, Tn. 37203
Name Mr & Mrs Paul Hugley
Address 3905 Wildeer Dr
Name Mrs. Wanda Smirnes
Address 2137 Imogene   Zip Code 38114
Name Mike & Gladys Keeton
Address 1713 Wisteria Denton, Tx. Zip Code 76201
Name Norma Lyle
Address Mike Gambill   Zip Code

One of several guest books from Elvis's funeral; note Caroline Kennedy's entry

LISA MARIE: It's hard to be in that place that my father was in. I think of Janis Joplin or Jim Morrison. I think of great artists who lost touch with reality. Artists who, for whatever reasons, surround themselves with people who help suck the life out of them. My father was a man who gave one too many rats to one too many snakes. When he started out, at a time when the Ku Klux Klan was still burning crosses, people thought he was black. He couldn't have cared less. He hung out at the blues clubs because the blues clubs had the music he liked. He sang in the style that he wanted to sing in. White people loved him, black people loved him, people who loved great music loved him. That's all that mattered.

PRISCILLA: It was an exquisite day, one of those California winter afternoons when the sun was mild and the air so crisp and clear you could see to the ends of the earth. I was up on Mt. Washington, at the peaceful retreat where Sri Daya Mata greeted her followers and continued her practice of spiritual enlightenment. She had graciously agreed to see me. After the ordeal of the elaborate funeral, after Lisa Marie,

Michelle and I had spent time in Europe trying to regain our footing, after so many sleepless nights and troubled days trying to process my feelings, I knew that she alone would understand.

As we sat in a shaded grove, she listened as my emotions poured out.

"You know, Priscilla," she said in her calm and reassuring voice, "when someone close to us dies at a time that seems premature, we can't help but feel some degree of guilt or responsibility. Why didn't we prevent it? Why didn't we do more for him? Why couldn't we have changed his fate so as to keep him alive? Well, the simple truth is that Elvis's spirit was powerful. It remains powerful. He was able to express that spirit throughout his life in ways that reached millions. That is cause for joy. The choices he made are the choices he made. But the choice we can now make is to gently move through our pain and confusion and celebrate his spirit. In a very real sense, he still lives. He always will."

Mountain Valley spring water, Elvis's favorite when he toured in the Seventies

Trunk of scarves, waiting to go on tour, August 1977

Elvis's wallet

One of the roses laid
on Elvis's coffin